I0089017

WILD
Witchcraft

OTHER BOOKS BY MARIAN GREEN

The Path Through the Labyrinth
Practical Techniques of Modern Magic
The Gentle Arts of Aquarian Magic
A Witch Alone
The Grail Seeker's Companion (with John Matthews)
Wild Witchcraft
Natural Witchcraft
Charms, Amulets, Talismans and Spells
An Introduction to Spiritual Ecology
The Treasure of the Silver Web

Marian Green has been the Editor of *Quest* quarterly magazine since 1970. This journal contains a variety of articles on all aspects of the Western Mystery Tradition, natural magic, divination and personal magical experience, as well as book reviews and news of conferences and events. Marian also runs several correspondence courses on Ceremonial and Natural Magic, holds workshops and gives talks and practical training to small groups throughout Britain and Europe.
She chooses not to use email, social media or the internet.

WILD
Witchcraft

A GUIDE TO NATURAL, HERBAL
AND EARTH MAGIC

Marian Green

Thoth Publications

Copyright © Marian Green 2023.
This edition published by Thoth Publications 2023.
First published as *The Elements of Natural Magic*
by Element Books, 1989.
Revised edition published by Thorsons, 2002.

Marian Green asserts the moral right to be identified as
the author of this work.

A CIP catalogue record for this book is available from
the British Library

All rights reserved. No part of this publication may be
reproduced, stored in a retrieval system, or transmitted,
in any form or by any means, electronic, mechanical,
photocopying, recording or otherwise, without the
prior permission of the publishers.

Cover design and text design by Helen Surman

Published by Thoth Publications
2 Copt Oak Cottage, Whitwick Road, Markfield,
Leicestershire LE67 9QB
ISBN 978-1-913660-41-3
Web address: www.thothpublications.com
Email: enquiries@thoth.co.uk

CONTENTS

DEDICATION

O Holy, Blessed Lady, constant comfort to humankind,
whose beneficence and kindness nourish us all,
and whose care for those in trouble is as a loving mother
who cares for all her children — you are there when we call.

THE GOLDEN ASS – Apuleius

PROLOGUE

THIS is a brief explanation about my theory of occult instruction. I have sometimes been asked why I don't write books on more advanced magic for those who have enjoyed the earlier works. After all, they say, I have been involved in occult work for nearly forty years, I must know some advanced techniques and rituals. True enough; yet I also know full well that there are three extremely good reasons for keeping such knowledge out of the books which untrained but enthusiastic students might read. These are my reasons:

1. All magical teachers are responsible for those they teach. Anyone who has spent many years studying and practising magic is fully aware of the dangers which entering occult work can involve. To teach the basic skills is fine, for when a student has mastered those he will be able to go on to tackle more advanced things. Within a school, each student is taught, under careful supervision, the level of magic he is capable of handling so that he cannot get out of his depth. With books, there is no guarantee that the unprepared

and unwary novice will not attempt, and succeed at, exercises over which he will have no control. I would not put an intelligent and keen child in charge of a fast car on a motorway. Although I might know that he could drive it safely around his garden, he would not have the strength, the awareness or the control to be safe anywhere else. I do teach magic at a higher level – but only face to face with students whose abilities and desires I know.

2. If you study the books on basic magical training and perform the exercises thoroughly – mastering the techniques and mental concentration required – the meditations which lead to that altered state of consciousness in which magic becomes a reality, will put you directly in touch with your own interior tutor. The Holy Guardian Angel or Higher Self will teach you all the magical work you can wish for, in a way that you can comprehend, and at a speed and level which is ideally suited to you. Merely copying someone else's 'Advanced Rite' or 'Grade Three Initiation' before you are ready will do you no good at all, and could genuinely harm you.

There are real dragons which you can encounter before you are adequately prepared to deal with them. When you can do all the basic things well – that is after at least two years' work – then you can ask your own contacts to teach you the higher levels of magic, or put you in touch with a school that will lead you onward. Each student can go as far as he wishes, either alone or under the direct instruction of a school, lodge, coven or other kind of group. If alone, he will first need to make a personal link with his Higher Self by hard, regular and effective practice.

3. Magical work is largely experiential. It is like swimming, riding a bike or playing a musical instrument: the more you do these things, the better you become at them, expanding your experience by actual practice. You cannot learn them just by reading the relevant books. Each person's experiences are different, both in ordinary life as well as in magical activities. As an example, take the simple act of entering the meditational state. The body is still and relaxed – fine – but then some feel light-headed and floating; others feel heavy; some feel hot; others feel buzzy and vibrational; some may clearly perceive pictures and hear words spoken to them inside their heads; others may see only vague shapes, or perhaps nothing at all, but they just 'imagine' things.

The varieties of experience at this level are endless. To describe all the possible experiences that a student at a higher level of working might encounter multiplies that complexity even more. It would mean either leaving a student in the dark by saying, 'enter state X using key H', which wouldn't mean very much, or writing pages of descriptive text, covering as many aspects of any state or symbol as have previously been encountered. Such books would be very boring. A teacher, looking at a small group of students, can see what they are experiencing and how far they are ready to go. She can see if any of them are getting into difficulties, are frightened or seem to be lost. By using her trained inner perception, the tutor will be able to detect these reactions immediately and help the students into calmer waters.

You can learn magical arts by being thrown in at the deep end; but this is neither ethical, nor in the end practical, for the nervous student will back away from the occult, accusing it of being 'evil' or 'mind-bending', simply because he has plunged in out of his depth, albeit often of his own choice. Although it may be over-cautious on my part, I prefer not to put those keys into the hands of unprepared novices, but to lead them along known roads until they encounter that aspect of their own inner being which can guide them safely to the stars.

Marian Green

INTRODUCTION

Mysterious energy triform, mysterious Matter, in fourfold and
sevenfold division: the interplay of which things weave the
Dance of the Veil of Life upon the Face of the Spirit.
Let there be harmony and beauty in your mystic loves.
MAGIC, IN THEORY AND PRACTICE – Aleister Crowley

O NE of the things said about modern life is that it
has 'lost its magic'. We mostly live in warm and
comfortable homes, have a wide selection of things to
do, plenty of different foods to eat, instant worldwide
communications and technologies which would have
been beyond imagination even fifty years ago, yet the
sense of wonder is often missing. It is for this reason that
many thinking people – from all walks of life and from
many lands across the world – are looking for 'some
thing else'. One of the aspects of their quest, which
in many cases is not merely on the material plane, is
a new spiritual dimension, a reaching outwards for
something that is hard to define, intangible and ethereal,
yet fascinating for all that. In part, this feeling is caused

by a longing for some kind of 'golden age' which seems to have passed, even though history tells us that life in previous ages was hard, uncomfortable and not half as glorious as we would like to imagine. Yet, the past holds a real clue to that which is being sought.

Other people, in this search for a new direction, have turned their attention to what they suppose is the simple life of the country; only to find the long hours of manual work in inclement weather are not as much fun as they seemed on the television! Village life can be lonely, the working of the land hard, its harvests fickle, the natives unfriendly and the production of all those succulent, organically grown vegetables tedious and heavy. Again, part of the answer does lie in the soil and its varied produce, but not in quite the same way that the seekers of self-sufficiency imagine.

The underlying theme, which may provide a fulfilment of the quest and an end to the search, concerns Nature. To those who have opted for a pagan answer she is Mother Nature, the Earth Goddess, Gaia or any of her other myriad names. Others have found their contentment by attuning themselves to the long-forgotten tides of Moon and season, Sun and sea, of land and circling stars. Both of these connections with the cog wheels of Creation have their roots in antiquity and within our own oldest inheritance. It is by rediscovering our magical links with the Wild World that we will be

INTRODUCTION

able to recover our kinship with the powers of Creation and re-creation.

The magic that seemed to be there for many people in childhood has not vanished, it is just that our adult eyes perceive things on a different wavelength to when we were children, and so the hidden paths of fairyland seem to have vanished for ever. If we are willing to re-open those clear-seeing eyes of childhood, consciously and carefully, we will all be able to re-awaken the vision which allowed magical things to happen. Each of us has retained the key to our past abilities, but we may well have forgotten where the lock is that will open it. Through the application of arts, skills and techniques we can restore our inherent powers to heal, to see into the future, to change our own lives and to make green again those wastelands, be they in the world around us or in our starved and lonely souls within.

The words 'Wild Witchcraft' might appear to be a contradiction in terms, but witchcraft is wild and Nature is magical. Magic is a power for change and has laws which can be used if particular rules are followed. In the past, in pre literate ages, magic was a normal part of many people's lives. Now we have the wonders of modern technologies, the real magic has been put to one side and forgotten. The only thing that stops most people from recognising the power of magic in their lives, and making use of its transforming energies, is a lack of experience. I say 'experience' – not belief – because you will not necessarily need to believe anything: you will come to know the reality of magic by experience if you are willing to make a few experiments, sincerely, carefully, and with an open mind.

There are always forces at work in our lives, our relationships, and in those ever-developing inner skills which we all take for granted. Magic is the art of learning to recognise these elements of change: the natural patterns of flow and ebb, the times of progress, of standing still and of retreating. Once these clearly determined currents are felt and appreciated, then their vast powers can be brought into our own use. Magic teaches us to determine which way the tides of Nature are flowing, to see on which level they run and what they can offer each of us at this moment.

By accepting that each of us is just as real a part of Nature as any tree, animal, ocean, plant or invisible life force, and being willing to rediscover skills that we had forgotten all about, anyone with a pinch of common sense, a fair share of determination and a sense of humour, can discover unexpected talents within themselves, once they are willing to acknowledge that they are there to be awakened. It is simply by re-establishing an understanding of Nature around us and by realigning our lives with those forces of change. that each of us may discover inner peace and tranquillity, new magical arts, ways of healing and self-awareness. We each need to recognise essentially who we are, where we are going and where we wish to go. By perceiving the tides of Nature and working with, rather than against them, we will all gain in confidence, health and satisfaction with life. By restoring some of the sense of wonder we had as children, and permitting ourselves to relearn our inherent magical skills, we may find shortly that our whole world has been changed for the better.

In each section of this book there are exercises, meditations and ancient arts described in ways that are acceptable to most modern people. You will not be required to leave your home and dwell in a hut in the woods in order to encounter Nature, nor will you need to pay vast sums of money for outlandish costumes and arcane equipment. You will need to dedicate a little time – each day if you are serious about your interest in Wild Witchcraft – to some kind of mental, spiritual or physical work, just as you would need to practise if you were learning to play the piano or taking up ski-racing. Magic takes time to master because its various skills and crafts exercise mental faculties and parts of your inner being that modern life scarcely touches. The early exercises may cause strange things to happen in your life, but that is simply the power of magic getting into gear and coming under your control. No one can guarantee that you will enjoy the first experiences, but the thrill of bringing more of life under your direct control will be worth any 'scary' moments at the beginning.

The hardest task is to persist, even if nothing is happening as far as you can tell, because at first you will literally be working with unseen forces within you. It does take a while before they work to your bidding. Keep at each and every art, craft and spiritual exercise for at least a month of regular practice and you will be amazed at what you have achieved by the end of that time. Try each thing only a few times, without dedication or application of will, and the results may be undetectable or totally unpleasant, upsetting your psychic or dream life and causing events to appear to be out of control. Keep at it, with patience and a sense of playfulness and soon you will really experience the power of magic within your own nature, and in life in general.

CHAPTER ONE

WORKING WITH NATURE

'Mother of fertility, on whose breast lieth water, whose cheek is
caressed by air, and in whose heart is the Sun's fire, womb of all
life, recurring grace of seasons, answer favourably the prayer.'
MAGIC, IN THEORY AND PRACTICE – Aleister Crowley

Probably the hardest thing we modern, technological people have to face is the reality of magic: that it is an invisible force which, like any other energy source, obeys certain laws and can be produced and controlled by those who know how to use it. Anyone, by personal dedication, study and practice, can learn its mastery. It is often an unperceived facet of our everyday lives, for the most obvious aspect of magic is that of change or transformation.

CHANGE AND TRANSFORMATION

It is in the service of change that all works of magic manifest themselves. Some of those changes occur to the 'magic-maker' or witch, some happen outside him or her to the physical world. All other changes take place on different levels of reality or in what might appear to us as other dimensions of time or space.

———

Our first step towards understanding what magic can do is to acknowledge change as a part of the world we all live in. No one can deny that they have changed since they were children; not only in physical shape, but also in mental attitudes, ideas and basic understanding. We may have changed our job, our partner or our home many times. Some of those changes will have come about because we made a decision to alter something and then went through the right stages in order to achieve it. Sometimes, other factors may cause changes which we have not set in motion ourselves, for example, the loss of a job through redundancy, the loss of a member of the family through death, or a change of home due to road improvements. You will be able to think of many examples in your own life.

The third sort of changes may not be so common. These are the transformations that you wish to take place, but appear to have no lever by which you can bring them about. That is where magic might well come into play. But magic is not the tool of greed, selfishness or covetousness, for everything you obtain by occult means has to be paid for, just as those ordinary things in your life cost money, effort or some kind of exchange. It is by grasping these basic concepts, which are parts of Nature – that arch-mistress of change (for she governs time, the Earth and its seasons) and by learning to work within a natural framework, that magic can be brought into your life.

———

MAGICAL SKILLS

Magic is an ancient aspect of our heritage, but many of its skills – being those of the mind and inner sight rather than the eye and hand of ordinary work – are not taught to us in schools. Most people who take up the practice and study of the occult arts usually do so at least as teenagers, and often as quite mature adults. All children have an appreciation of the laws of magic, but once they go to school, start to learn to read and cope with the world around them, they have little time for the unseen which they knew so well before. Beginning to study such a vast and intricate subject, which spans much of mankind's evolution on Earth and is found in every land, religion and culture, is no easy task. Often, seeing only an overview, some students are deterred from ever starting on the practical work. Nevertheless, although the entire subject is enormous, many parts of it are both simple, and within our daily reach. These are the frequently overlooked arts of natural magic.

Since the 1950s there has been an increasing interest and awareness in the old ways – many books on different approaches to the occult, divination and witchcraft have been written or reprinted, and the market appears to be continuing to expand. We all have a longing to explore the unseen, a fascination with the future, a curiosity about other kinds of beings or different dimensions of reality. Somehow we know they exist, yet seemingly have no magic key with which to open any doors to the strange realms which we might encounter beyond.

However, it is really a lack of knowledge, rather than a lack of either key or door, for both are within easy reach once you know where to look for them. Both are to be found within your 'inner self', that is, the levels of your unconscious mind which are usually only discovered during dreams and day-dreams. Dion Fortune, one of England's greatest magical women, wrote, '*Magic is the art of causing changes in consciousness according to the will...*' and that simple statement is the most important concept in the appreciation of all the magical arts. Learn to control and change your consciousness, your perceptions on several levels, and you can change the entire universe.

In everyday life we think of perhaps two conditions of consciousness – being awake or being asleep – we do not recognise generally that there are many gently graded stages between those fairly clear states. The first arts of magical work, in both Eastern and Western traditions, recognise these intervening states. Meditation and mind-training exercises gradually grant control of these states, so that the practitioner may enter the level of consciousness which aligns with the level of perception required for magic.

It is an extremely simple thing to say; but then it might seem quite easy to describe how to play the piano by just putting your fingers on the keys and pressing. Everyone recognizes that it is not quite as simple as that! Mastering the changes in perception whilst keeping these under control is actually very difficult. It requires both relaxation and attention, a serious objective and a playful mood; yet once you have managed to strike the right balance, it is not hard and gets more and more interesting once the basic technique is mastered.

Like most of the practical arts and crafts of magic, if they are properly applied, they are safe, useful and beneficial in a wide variety of ways. When taken up by foolish people, however, trying to gain 'instant enlightenment', these gentle arts can be dangerous and destructive. In magic a little knowledge can be a dangerous thing, but if you always apply common sense and take your explorations or inner journeys slowly, venturing step by careful step into the hidden places of your mind, you will always be able to cope with whatever turns up. That is not to say that you will enjoy every stage, or that you may not be frightened, unsettled or confused by what happens to you. If you are serious about your interest, then the forces of the inner worlds will treat you gently, but if you barge into their subtle levels, demanding help, gain or changes which are purely selfish, you will be in for a rough and unpleasant ride.

The forces of magic move the entire galaxies in their courses, and when you first get in among them they

_____

can shake you up and twist you round, just as if you were going through some kind of massive launderette machine. In one sense you probably are doing just that, for cleansing and purification have always been early stages in the practices of both religious and occult work.

NATURE – BOTH INNER AND OUTER

In the study of witchcraft you will need to begin by looking at Nature. If you are intending to use the forces of the tides and seasons you will need to explore these, appreciate them on more than just a superficial level, and immerse yourself in their amazing currents until they are familiar and comfortable. There are lots of people who claim to be witches or shamans, but who do not have the slightest idea what the moon phase is or which way the tides of the seasons are running. In their 'Book of Shadows' (the handwritten book of dreams, rituals and spells kept by every witch) a lot of space is given over to the words of rituals to be performed in honour of the Goddess of the Moon or Earth, celebrating her power or story, yet ignoring what she is actually doing outside the building – inside which, inevitably, the witches are performing their rite. It is a much better, safer and more exhilarating experience to be out there, under a bright Moon, watching falling stars flash across the dark sky in answer to your prayers.

Nature has all the answers; she is our mother for, like

everything in the visible universe, we are all parts of one another. We are the stuff of stars; our atoms, which we have taken in with our food, are the same atoms which came out of the Creation of the Worlds! Every tree, plant, animal, jewel and other person shares this ancient heritage. Nature may, over the millennia, change one thing into another, for she is mistress of arcane alchemy, but in due time all things return to her and are recycled. Because we are essentially part of Nature, we have a kinship with all parts of Creation. It is this link which helps us to change things around us, and also to permit us to be changed by forces over which, for the time being, we have little control. We cannot actually cease to age, although for vanity's sake, we can cheat and try to prevent this natural process showing. We can pretend to be older, or different to how we actually are, but that will be of little benefit to us in the long term, or in our magical work.

Not only do we need to learn to acknowledge that we are part of Nature, but we absolutely have to find out who we are, what advantages and disadvantages we might have, what forgotten or overlooked skills and talents may be there. That is one of the hardest exercises of any form of magic, yet it is the key to our ultimate strength as a person and power as a magician: to be completely aware of our existing characteristics and of our potential skills is a vital step in the acquisition of arcane abilities.

All good schools of magic will insist that during the first part of their training all students look closely at who they are, where they have come from and where they think they are going to. This form of psychoanalysis is painful; it is intended to be thorough and is essential to anyone setting out upon the inner paths.

If you are studying alone or with a group of friends, you will each have to make these inner assays into your personal history, character, needs and ambitions. The best way is the use of a secret diary. It must be secret, for you will find it very hard to be absolutely honest if you believe that someone else will read it. It is never supposed to be a boastful document, confessing faults and failings to an amazed audience who might be astounded by your frank confessions, for that too is a false premise under which to perform this act of self evaluation.

It is important to take time over this: look back through your life, noting the successes and failures, from the earliest moments in your memory to yesterday. Think of your early ambitions and aims in life, see what you have made of them. How many of the things you really enjoyed as a child have long been put aside? How much joy might you derive from those simple pleasures if you took them up again now? Are you still influenced by your family's attitudes, their ideas and standards, or have you developed your own ethical codes? How have your aims changed? What started your current interest in magic? What are you going to do about it?

The other aspect, which it is important to look at, is your own relationship with Nature. On the simplest level, this is a matter of looking at whether or not you enjoy working in the garden, walking in the country, and if you see trees and plants as living beings, rather than nice green lumps in the landscape. How do you feel about herbs and flowers? Do they merely flavour your food or brighten up a dull corner of the house, or do you see them as living and healing entities with great powers to restore your zest for living?

How do you feel about the animal kingdom? Do you 'own' any pets or keep larger animals for pleasure or profit? What are your views on a vegetarian diet, wearing fur coats, modern farming methods and field sports? If you take up the practice of natural magic you will need to look long and hard at all of these factors, for you cannot ignore them and pretend they do not matter. If you expect to receive help or guidance from Mother Nature you are going to need to be able to express your feelings on these, and many other matters.

THE ELEMENTS
If you seriously intend to approach the Old Religion or take up our heritage of arcane knowledge, another deeper aspect of your current life which will need to be examined in detail is that of how you relate to the elements at large. How do you personally respond to the tides of the sea or any tidal river? Are you aware of the

phases of the Moon? Do they pattern your dreams? Do you enjoy being out in the sunshine and the rain? Which season do you prefer and which do you like least?

Each of these attitudes and inner feelings is prompted by your association with Nature all around you, usually unseen and unsensed, or taken for granted. When you begin your first tentative steps in the direction of the mastery of Wild Witchcraft, you will find all this vaguely seen and sensed data suddenly taking on a new dimension of importance and power. Once you set out into Nature's own realm you will encounter many fascinating and strange things, most of which stem from the inner links you already have with the world of Nature about you. If those links are weak or under-developed, it will take time and effort to make them strong enough to bear the brunt of the work you will do.

We are becoming a sensually deprived people, we who dwell in cities and have our being among man-made objects. We do not feel the wind and rain upon our faces, we do not watch the ever-changing glimmers of the stars, we do not walk in the wide, wild places of the spirit and sense the powers of the Old Gods in their habitations. We do not touch the Earth, the trees' rough bark, the leaves' velvet surfaces. It is only in the dreams of an unspent childhood that we can paddle in a sparkling stream of water that is fresher than bottled mineral water, play with wild animals, talk to trees, fly high like kites in unspoiled azure skies of endless summer days: or is it? If we are willing to cast off the dark cloak of ordinary sight, turn away from the convenience of having everything made easy for us and find those overlooked aspects of the inner wilderness which lie all about our towns and cities, there we may find the Gates to the Otherworld.

Nature has hidden her secret entrances to the place where dreams come true (for it is the place where dreams come from). Nevertheless, if we acknowledge her power and presence – albeit unsensed in ordinary terms – we can travel into that lost land and dwell there for a short space of time, to recharge our spiritual batteries, learn something of her undying wisdom and become, more effectively, whatever it is we want to become.

We must first begin to attune to those senses we have forgotten about; learn to see what is actually all around us, before we are able to perceive those paradoxical beings from other worlds. We must retrain our hearing to listen for fairy music heard above the din and clatter of the mundane world, for the music of the spheres is real and cannot be out-blasted by the worldly cacophony. We must learn to feel anew, not only with our bared nerves, but also with our hearts and inner senses. We need to appreciate the feelings of those around us, especially our nearest and dearest ones, for much of what they really wish to communicate is not in words, or even

---

overt gestures. We need to discover, just a little, the basic feelings of others we encounter on our daily round, to sense their fears and distrust, their hopes and desires from moment to moment.

The most obvious need is to learn to appreciate our environment, hear what the trees are saying, what the wind is whispering in our ears, what the clouds are foretelling of the weather to come. These things all seem real to most children, although adults mostly consider such notions to be childish – yet it is from these intangible sources of ancient data that the Old Wise Ones drew their knowledge and foreknowledge of what was to be. They certainly had magical powers, for they were closely attuned to the patterns of Nature and she would assist them in their abilities to heal, to discover the lost, console the lonely and magically change the future.

Once you can appreciate that there is a natural pattern within the whole of life, and see how it can be fitted closely into your own pattern of hopes and wishes, then the vast forces of Creation will begin to flow as you would wish them to from the microcosmic to the macrocosmic level. Much of natural magic is common sense, but that sense too has been eroded by modern living, where decision-making has often been taken out of our hands, and so much of our lives is shaped by the conditions we live in, the State and the authorities.

We have lost a great deal of our freedom; not that it has been seized from us by anarchic powers, but because we have forgotten how to choose, how to decide what we want and how to get it. It is only when we are jolted out of our unaware state by a sudden realisation about, and an appreciation of, the occult, for example, that the whole pattern and situation of our lives come sharply into focus, and force us to re-assess our position.

Taking up any new study is bound to have repercussions in our home and family life, whether it is joining some kind of sports or educational club or developing an interest in what many people consider to be an unhealthy, weird or downright evil subject. Despite the public's distrust of occult matters, there is an ever-growing number of serious and committed people, in all parts of the world, devoting their spare time to discovering answers to those eternal questions.

A mundane existence does not even consider questions regarding the meaning of life; Where are we going? What are we here for? What can be done to improve matters? Those questions may be examined in some detail by religious teachers, but the answers, being on the whole of a very personal nature, have to be sought individually. The occult path – leading as it does through the unseen and unexplored regions of our inner being – not only accepts the validity of the questions, but also goes a long way, if we allow it, towards discovering the answers to each question in turn.

———

THE BALANCE OF NATURE

Magic is an energy source. It is neutral in force, like time and the tides, but the way it is used can be either beneficial or destructive. In every situation where magic is used, it is important for the practitioner to verify his reasons and objectives before setting those mysterious forces to work. Every action has an equal and opposite reaction, as every student of physics knows, but this same law applies in magic too.

We prefer to ignore the forces of decay and dissolution because we do not usually control them, but they play a critical part in all of our lives. Both are vital to our continuance on this planet, for without decay nothing would be recycled. All waste matter, wherever it came from, would simply pile up and the whole world would soon be buried. Take a look at the average town's ever-growing rubbish dump and you get some idea of the problem. In your lifetime, that would probably be the amount of rubbish you would produce on your own if it were all piled up in one place. However, Nature sets the forces of change to work upon it; bacteria, time and decay work their way through the organic refuse, eating it away, turning it into compost, gases, humus and its basic chemicals. It is then ready to be used as new plant food, animal fodder or, through the washing agency of rain, to be swept out to sea, where in time it will again produce sediments, chemicals and minerals which plate movements may return to the surface in the ages to come.

Left alone and working with organic materials, Nature can, in due time, balance and recycle everything. What has happened now, however, is that mankind has interfered and created new, impervious materials which will not decay. Technology has changed the balance of our effects upon those parts of the Earth's mantle that we can get at and make use of. We extract minerals, gems, coal, oil, clay, rare earths, water and even the rocks beneath our feet, as if all these things were a growing and renewable resource. We live in a world in which the forests, untouched for thousands of years, are vanishing week by week. The woodlands are Nature's handkerchief, mopping up the tears of rain and releasing them gradually in a steady drying out process. Remove the hanky, and all the valuable water rushes down the bare mountainsides, carrying off the precious topsoil and its fertility, blocking rivers, causing landslides and killing fish in the seas with the mud and debris. One careless action, for immediate gain, will destroy the balance of Nature. One careless act of magic, without a thought to the possible consequences, can have just as devastating an outcome, unless those engaged in magical work watch what they are doing.

At a more basic level – and closer to home — we need to look at what we might be doing that is detrimental to

---

our environment, not necessarily with our own hands, but by our desire to be fashionable or to improve what is acceptable to a higher level. A new front door might add value to our house, but it might well be made from ancient hardwood trees cut down in one of the dying forests. One door might not be much, but others in the street might want them too, so more trees go, and more trees are used for window frames, for interior decoration, for lavatory seats. Is that moral? Is it necessary to pillage Mother Nature in order to set a destructive trend? That is the first question which must be answered if you really wish to follow the Old Ways. What am I doing in my life through thoughtlessness, carelessness or ignorance that might have far reaching consequences for the world, my children or those in distant lands?

INCREASED AWARENESS

It is important that we become aware of our every mundane and magical act. Where does the food I eat today come from? How was it grown, and who was deprived that this food might be exported to another land? It can be a hard question, and the answer can very often cause ripples of discomfort to begin to flow through what had seemed to be an innocent and caring lifestyle. Nature is bountiful. She can replace much of that which is destroyed if she is given the time and the opportunity. However, once we have interfered, then she cannot work to rebuild those carefully balanced and interlinked structures of growth, decay and stability. No matter how strong our desire to help, no matter how powerful our skills at magic, we cannot lift a finger to restore the deserts, heal the wastelands, make green the bare rockfaces that not so long ago were impenetrable jungle. Those things, at that level of change, need to be the works of those Immortal Beings: Time, Nature and the rest. The level at which we can help is much smaller and nearer to home.

We will all need to regain our awareness of the phases of Nature, our feelings of the seasons and the cyclic changes each of those brings to the inner levels of our lives. We need to know the powers of the Moon, with her waxing and waning face, and shifting dance across the skies of night. We need to understand the healing forces of the Sun and his bright protecting energy, his enlivening and fertilizing light within our outward lives. We will have to learn what his circling pattern tells us, as within our personal horoscope, his energy sweeps across the other planets, enhancing and encouraging the varying aspects of our individual natures. We need to adjust to the actual seasons, the growing, sowing, reaping and cleansing tides that change our ways of thinking, both inwardly and outwardly, although few untrained individuals are aware at what level some of these forces work.

On other levels, we will need to look at human nature, how people reflect the designs of the Eternal, how individuals work with or against the tides of the world. We may need to study aspects of the real world, its herbs and healing plants; the powers of gems, rocks and crystals; the energies of 'ley lines'. those hidden veins of the Earth's own energy streams detected by dowsing. We have to understand the weather, the winds and tides for, subtle though their effects may be, working with them will make many aspects of our ordinary existence much easier and smoother.

We each have various tasks to fulfil, from incarnation to incarnation, and if we understand what these might be, it is easier to accomplish them. Our relationships matter, and the way we can interact with other folk, through love or tolerance, through trust or respect, and we ought to understand how they feel about us. All these subtle senses can be woken up if we permit ourselves to be more relaxed and natural.

There are many magical arts: some are very old, especially those being rediscovered under the title of shamanism; others are more recent in their provenance – like homoeopathy, for example, a very specialised healing art based on the uses of minute doses of natural minerals, herbs and other substances. Although herbalism requires a fair amount of book-learning, it is by developing the inner arts of intuition and subtle sensing that most forms of therapy are applied when it comes to the practical side of the work.

You do need to study pictures and intuitively match them with the powers or 'virtues' of every medicinal plant, tree or flower, knowing for certain that you have the right one, and the right part of it to be used for that form of treatment.

You also have to recognise the effect the seasons have upon the use of healing plants. For example, in winter you will need to rely on dried leaves or roots, for you cannot expect Nature to supply you with fresh flowers in January! This may be a small and seemingly obvious point, but there are people around who, having become used to constant heat and light inside buildings, forget that the winter is out there, stripping the greenery from the bare branches, killing the grasses and putting the perennial herbs to sleep within the earth.

Even in summer it is not always possible to pick precisely the stem or flower that you need, for plants flower early or late, bear leaves before or after blossoming, or provide less of the required healing substance in droughts or wet weather. Today we can find out about these varying factors from books or the internet, but in the end, we still have to find the places where the plants thrive in the wild, or in those specially cultivated places under human control. We have to have knowledge to differentiate deadly hemlock from tasty parsley when each plant is just emerging in the spring. We need to understand that on chalk or in clay soils, certain plants will or will not be found. We need to know the powers of the rocks below whose energies determine which kinds of trees flourish in what part of our familiar landscape.

We have to learn all these things which our forebears knew because they had grown up close to the land, knowing almost instinctively what might be found where and the healing properties it would have. Only a couple of generations have passed, yet much of the information those people knew, especially those living closest to nature in the countryside, has been lost because it seemed unimportant to a technological society. Now we are beginning to acknowledge the loss of this simple and basic wisdom, we are having to take complicated steps to relearn things which would have been common knowledge only a hundred years ago. It is very hard work too, and that is only a tiny part of the necessary instruction for a would-be Wild Witch.

EXPLORING THE INNER REALMS

The other aspects largely involve developing the powers of the mind; not merely the memory which recognises plants, stones, jewels, symbols, clouds, planets or messages on the wind, but the mind which also knows what to do with them. We each have to explore who we are, where we are going, what we desire to achieve, and then discover which path through the maze of human consciousness leads closest to our chosen direction. Although learning all the outer material seems hard, those varied exercises which open inner doors and teach us to control them are often much harder. In the outer world you will have standards which others can recognise. You can demonstrate your knowledge, for example, by listing useful herbs, but on the inner levels there are no clear signposts, no useful reference books, only your bare intuition in its undeveloped form.

To explore the inner realms of consciousness, you must walk into unmapped territory and you will have to travel alone through those hidden landscapes until you know them as well as you do the ordinary world. You will need to set aside a time and a place in which you can seek the stillness. You will also need the courage to set aside your ordinary waking consciousness and freely enter another, unfamilar state, wherein you can see the unseen, appreciate those inner aspects of your own being and little by little start to feel secure.

Gradually you will come to terms with what might seem to be dreamscapes and discover characters there who will offer guidance or help, healing and control of magical forces. You can decide for yourself if these are 'real'; whether they are merely parts of you or if they have a separate existence and are there when you are not in their world to watch them. In whatever way you come to appreciate the beings you encounter on your journeys (I will tell you how to begin in another chapter), you must treat them with respect and honour, for whatever they may actually be, they are powerful and can disrupt your journeys, frighten you or interfere with your sleep. They can show you how to master the ancient arts, they can teach you divination, and they can lead you to the sources of interior wisdom which have always been there waiting for you to discover in the way that your simple, land-loving ancestors did only a few generations ago.

Time is our greatest enemy. We never seem to have enough of it and yet the number of time and energy saving devices that exist within our life spheres is growing all the time. Magic requires quite a lot of it, separated from ordinary life to begin with, but once the ancient arts are mastered, they blend invisibly with the rest of our life and we tend to use our inner powers almost all the time. Initially, however, it is necessary to deliberately set aside time every day, come what may, to practise, study and relearn those things we all knew as children. Without regular practice nothing will work and the disruptions which can be caused, once a few chinks in the sealed door to interior wisdom are opened, can be very unpleasant. It is necessary, even at the very start of your magical adventures, to make a firm commitment and a personal dedication to continue – at least for a couple of years!

CHAPTER TWO

HERB, TREE AND PLANT LORE

'0 circle of Stars, whereof our Father is the youngest brother,
marvel beyond imagination, soul of infinite space, before whom
Time is ashamed, the mind bewildered, and the understanding
dark, not unto Thee may we attain, unless Thine image be Love.
Therefore by seed and root and stem and bud and leaf and flower
and fruit do we invoke Thee ...'

MAGIC, IN THEORY AND PRACTICE – Aleister Crowley

Our first task, if we are to make any sense at all of Wild Witchcraft, is seriously to re-assess our relationship with the earth beneath our feet and Mother Nature, the Earth Mother who freely gives of her bounty. Unless we are willing to respect, love and honour the Earth as a vast living entity, any magic using her forces is a waste of time. We are all living in a crucial era – the Earth is threatened and mankind can easily become an endangered species through his own folly, greed and insatiable desire to possess things. We can no longer use ignorance as an excuse. The media, in the last few years, has been increasingly filled with pictures, articles, documentary films and explanations as to what is happening to the land and the rivers, the seas and the now polluted skies. We have no excuse. Although each of us might feel we are in no way responsible for this destructive approach to Nature, in fact each of us is, in part, responsible for what is happening all around us.

It is for each of us to make a new and individual dedication to do whatever is possible to redress the balance and assist Nature to restore those things which have not been eroded too far to be redeemable. We may certainly work within the confines of the ordinary world – planting trees, collecting rubbish, recycling waste and joining practical campaigns – but those who take the magical road have other tasks. There are many areas within the inner worlds where a little concerted effort can be the cause of vast and beneficial changes in the exterior world. Magic works at the root of transformation and at the growing point of all new enterprises. By setting something in motion, using the energy available at any time of change, it is possible to transform things on a far greater scale than an individual or group could hope to do, working in the outer world alone.

ANCIENT ARTS

In the past, those who knew the sacred Magic of Nature were the ordinary country folk, going about their tedious tasks in field and farmyard: sowing, reaping, gathering, picking up stones and spreading manure.

Their days were determined by the Sun's hours in the sky during the day and the Moon's phases at night. They toiled hard and reaped small benefit from their labours, yet they probably had a certain degree of peace and contentment, something which is so often missing in our civilized and convenient modern situations. Within each community, each family or individual had a place. They would gain vast stores of intricate knowledge from the people around them in the village or town about its traditional crafts and industries. Some had the added dimension of learning the Crafts of the Wise and would specialise in folk magic using the herbs, stones, trees and sacred objects which Nature provided for all her children. Many of these ancient skills have seemingly vanished for ever because the whole pattern of life in rural areas has changed. However, many of them have simply sunk back into the levels of time-past, and within that memory store, remain in safe-keeping until modern adventurers enter those forgotten places and recall the wisdom resting there.

Much of the old talent for magic ran in families or clans, like the ability to work with horses, have 'green fingers' with plants or be 'weather wise'. Magic requires a wide variety of abilities, partly on a mental level (for an excellent memory is vital to being able to create proper spells on the spur of the moment), and partly on a practical level. It is no good knowing how to make a particular talisman if you do not have the ability to actually design, carve, paint, embroider or mould it when it is needed. You also need to know what certain materials are good for and how to make use of ordinary objects, for many of the traditional charms are simply stones, twigs or pieces of wood imbued by Nature with some special power, and recognised as such by any natural magician.

THE VALUE OF TREES

As an example, nearly all trees have a particular energy which they may share with us. Some are clearly healing trees, others offer strength, or calmness, or a kind of sparkling vitality which our jaded spirits may absorb from them. Trees have mighty guardian spirits, called by some Dryads or Hamadryads, and these can assist with empowering talismans if you have made contact with them and are willing to ask for their help.

Other trees are used in a variety of herbal medicines, from the most basic infusions of leaves or the decoctions of bark from trees like the willow – from which salicylic acid (aspirin) is derived – to the delicate yet powerful Bach Flower Remedies. In the latter case, Dr Bach, an English physician, discovered that the virtue or healing essence of certain flowers or trees could be extracted and preserved in a solution which could be effectively used as a medicine. Using the very ancient method of floating flowers in spring water, he allowed the Sun's rays to infuse the secret virtue of 38 different plants to become what are now known as the Bach Flower Remedies. These very special solutions work with a genuinely magical power on all those conditions of mind or spirit which conventional medicine does not even recognize, let alone attempt to treat. Bach Remedies work on fears, anxieties, intolerance, mental phases, transitions in life, confusion, pain, loss or exhaustion. From common trees like oak, elm, pine, chestnut, larch and crab apple, a wide variety of gentle healing essences are extracted. These work, not so much on the body, but on the mind and spirit. Their effects can seem miraculous to those who have long been sunk into unremitting depression or who suffer from tension, indecision or anguish. Some work immediately, bringing calm after a shock or accident, like the famous Rescue Remedy; others may bring sleep or gradual peace of mind, perhaps taking a whole lunar cycle before their curative effect is noticed. Other countries have developed their own local flower and tree remedies based on the same principles. Bach Remedies are available worldwide though!

Trees have had an important part to play in the magical systems of the West. The ancient Druid priests, whose only temples were beneath the branches of the trees in their sacred groves, may well have even derived their name from that of the oak tree. They were magicians, astrologers, law-givers and healers, and though the modern Orders of Druids – who may be seen celebrating the solar festivals in public places – have very tenuous links with their mystic forebears, they have at least preserved some of their ideas. The ancient Celtic people named the letters of their Ogham alphabet after trees and probably sent messages, in the summer at least, by threading different leaves to spell them out on a twig which could be sent to another, who could then interpret the content easily.

A complicated form of divination and foreseeing was also based on the magical meaning of about twenty different indigenous trees. These 'Talking Twigs' or 'Bardic Lots' were a hand-span long, about as thick as the end of the diviner's little finger and had their top and bottom ends marked by the way they were cut and rounded, so you could judge 'heads' or 'tails'. The bundle of thin, straight twigs was shaken in a cylindrical container, probably carved from the diviner's 'totem' tree, which was the tree that was specially sacred to their family, and as the twigs fell out upon a special white cloth, the pattern they made and how they touched or crossed each other would be interpreted in a similar way to a tarot card spread. As the twigs were shaken together, they would make a lovely chattering noise and a sort of clink as they landed upon other dry sticks.

In the past, many people's surnames were derived from their totem tree. Look through any telephone directory, for example, to discover how many folk are called Ashwood, Oakley, Hornbeam, Holly, Firman, Sloegrove, Blackwood and the like. There are many woody derivatives too: Hedger, Groves, Woodley, Forester, Bodger, Carver, Turner and Barker, showing how many country occupations were concerned with wood and trees. Perhaps your own family name is in someway related to woodwork or the forests which, in Celtic times, covered a great deal more of Britain and Europe than they do now.

Wood was an important magical substance. It was recognized very early on that it had the property of floating on water, and it is thought that the vast stones for such monuments as Stonehenge, were carried on rafts – some a few miles from the Marlborough Downs, others all the way from the Preseli Mountains in South Wales. Boats, houses, furniture and spears, bows and arrows were all aspects of the Wood Age. A huge circular temple building was erected at Woodhenge, which predates Stonehenge, so it is no wonder that part of our magical heritage is concerned with the specialised use of wooden objects like wands and platters. Even modern magicians pay a slight homage to this past wisdom by retaining the wand as their Rod of Power, just as it is seen on the tarot cards, and which in some old designs is still sprouting leaves and twigs.

A stick was probably the first tool of evolving humanity, picked up to knock ripe fruits from a high branch and later to carry fire from a lightning struck tree to the first fireplace. Fire hardened the staff, straightened its kinks, sharpened a point and provided an arrow or spear to reach beyond the hunter's arm. Other sticks, in who knows what ancient time, were found to act as divining rods, twisting in the hands of the sensitive ones to indicate underground water, or the direction of a spring among rocks. Later on, this same basic technology was used to find minerals, gold and oil, as it is by some diviners to this day.

Trees are powerful symbols found in nearly all religions and ancient philosophies: sometimes as the Tree of Life, and sometimes as the Tree of Knowledge of Good and Evil. Once you open your eyes to what is so clearly depicted in historical records, you can see that carvings and religious paintings from India, Egypt, Persia, Chaldea, Babylon, Scandinavia and all over Europe depict sacred trees as symbols of eternal life, axes of the world, preservers of wisdom, protectors of prophets from the heat of the Sun and much more.

In Britain, the tree hides the God of Nature, the Earth Mother's consort. Look around ancient cathedrals and churches and see amid the carvings of the roof bosses green men, foliate heads, and human faces with leaves, flowers and vines emerging from the mouth, hair and beard. Here is the Old God, hidden in the buildings of the incoming Christian Church, showing that the Old Religion would still have its representatives among the newer symbolism. Seek out the Lady, too; disguised, as was her wont, as a doe, a hare, a cat, an owl, a lily or a rose. Look up at the construction of these old village churches and see how the vaulting is designed to look like the branches of trees, spreading from the stone pillar trunk, often to provide nests for resting angels, fauns, tree spirits, animals sacred to the church's forerunners, and all the foliage which so clearly indicates the surviving aspects of the former tree worship. If the congregation was made to come in from the rain and from their shelter under the canopy of sacred forest glades, then they managed to import much of the familiar symbolism onto the fabric of the stone buildings. The masons, with their secret arts of stone carving, also brought the sacred symbols of an undying faith, which perhaps they shared. After all, in their own initiation myth, the reviving architect is discovered under an acacia tree!

We cannot usually lose ourselves within the Wild Wood these days, but we can learn something of its power and impact upon our inner lives by re-creating it within our interior vision. First we must get to know the trees, each different, each imbued with strange energies and healing, before we can learn to tap into these. Examine the world around you. There are bound to be all sorts of trees, even in the inner cities. Go and really see them, examine their bark, feel the power which seeps or rushes up or down their trunks. Smell the leaves, listen to the branches and leaves talking in the wind, taste the air about them, see if you can spot the flowers and developing fruits. Find out what sort they are, how long they live, what the wood is used for and its magical name. Interact with a fine and healthy tree, show it to your children, picnic at its foot or hug it for consolation. Choose a tree and dance around it; never mind if you are grown up. If anyone questions your action say its your birthday, or that all your family talk to trees! Be willing to cast off the conventions which differentiate between people and aspects of Nature, for remember, the trees are made of star-stuff, so that makes them your relations, for you are created of star-stuff too!

Once you have got to know a few real trees, or a forest full, if that is possible, you will then be able to create an inner doorway into the Wild Wood, where adventures may happen and much natural magic has its roots. The wilderness which is inside each of us is a place of formation, and there dwell the elements of all the changes and developments we wish to make in our lives. Within that inner realm are all the aspects of our individual creativity, our artistic, musical, poetic and literary talents, our inventiveness and our abilities to cope, to learn and to evolve. Most of us never venture into those shadowy depths and encounter these parts of ourselves. Normally we would only half-see them in dreams or sense them echoed in good books.

In our modern world a wood or forest might be an unfamiliar concept. Yet it is another part of our unrecognised magical heritage, which is shared by Europe, South and North America. Within that untamed jungle are the keys to all the things we desire to become, to obtain and to achieve through magical work – if we choose to commit ourselves to that entangled path. It is a 'place between the worlds', of past and future, of inner and outer, of magic and 'reality'. Within those shady walks and hidden glades are to be found the huts of our shaman ancestors and the Halls of the Sacred Kings, long ago sacrificed upon the tree, yet living still where neither time nor tide can touch them. Here is the abode of the Goddess, Gaia, the Earth Mother, and all the Goddesses of Sacred Springs of Inspiration, and the Cauldron or Grail. Here, the Oracles still dwell, now that Delphi and Ephesus are given over to the tourist hoards. Here are all the Elemental Beings in their own realms of Earth, Water, Fire and Air, where we can meet them, face to face, for they have long since hidden in the teeming lands of Earth.

STORY-TELLING AND INNER JOURNEYS

Each of us has the hidden key which will open the gate to these interior realms. It is the way to use it that has usually been forgotten. The method is one we may well have been familiar with as children, for it is the art of story-telling. In the East the method of escaping the mundane world is often that of chanting, adopting tense postures, counting each breath and concentrating on mandala patterns. In the West we have a different approach that is becoming another forgotten strand in our heritage of wisdom. The hero tales, the myths and legends are not a

---

mere form of entertainment from the days before radio and television, they are encoded programs, working on aspects of our inner minds which have the power to set free our imagination, vision and clear sight of things from other times, both past and future.

Within each traditional tale there is a master plan, and if you learn to hear not only the words, but the secret message concealed therein, you will begin to understand that you can use these ancient stories to open up deeply buried aspects of your own consciousness. The characters of each legend represent aspects of our own characters or figures we will meet, both in the world around us and within the hidden realms. Carl Jung called them 'Archetypes' and listed many of the traditional figures from ancient tale or myth: the Old Wise Woman (or witch in many fairy stories), the Hero, the Child, the Virgin/Mother, and many more. Each of these represents someone we might encounter on our inner journeys, or seek out for help or healing. Each of them is also an overlooked aspect of our true and complex selves, which may be the hardest concept to understand.

By using the ancient bardic art of story-telling, and entering fully into that land of myth, the mind is gently led away from mundane cares until, without its noticing or protesting, that subtle change of consciousness leading into a contemplative state takes over. It does take effort, concentration and regular practice, combined with a desire to succeed to make this simple exercise effective, but it is built into the tradition of natural magic and will generally work well for students.

Today, instead of having the travelling story-teller visit our homestead and sing his tales accompanied by harp tunes, we use the modern equivalent – your chosen digital device, or analogue tape-recorder. Now there are many well-recorded and carefully scripted inner journeys with music or sound effects, designed specifically to lead the listener into those other worlds of experience and wisdom. Using the language of symbolism – so much more potent than mere descriptive words – the listener is gently led away from his familiar surroundings into one of the aspects of the inner realms.

To create these narratives it is always necessary for the story-teller or writer to actually go into those different planes of existence, enter the Wild Wood and describe what he encounters there. Often when an inner journey is being heard you will find yourself a few steps ahead, yet you get to each of the described places or meet the inhabitants of those levels just as they are depicted in the narrative. This helps you to know that you have actually entered that realm and that what you are experiencing is real, within that context. It is always important to keep to the path described, however, for the easiest way to get lost is to ignore instructions, stop, or seemingly turn off. From then on you are on your own, and what you encounter may not be helpful, or might seem frightening. It really is important that you carefully examine your own vision of each stage as it comes up, be it a character, place or object and concentrate, in a relaxed way on that single point. It might help you to repeat silently what is being said to you and use all your imaginative powers to conjure that particular image clearly before your mind's eye. If you practise with simple narratives, learning the general trend so that you can work through them, a bit at a time, with your eyes closed, and your body comfortably relaxed, you will get the hang of the method quite quickly.

To begin any journey you will need to prepare a few things first. You will need a comfortable but supportive upright chair in a place where you will not be disturbed for at least half an hour. It is no good slumping on your bed, for that is programmed in your subconscious as a place where you go to sleep, and it is hard not to! It is better for your breathing and circulation that you sit upright, with your spine supported and resting in its natural curves. Your head should be kept up, and you will find that you can relax completely and still keep your head up. Relax your neck, face and shoulders by tensing each in turn and then letting it go limp. Work down through your whole body, carefully sensing inside any areas of tension and discomfort. Make sure you feel calm and ready to begin your journey. Breathe slowly and deeply for a few minutes, breathing out tension or worry and inhaling energy and clear inner sight. For a training session, follow the path described here or one with similar images. Close your eyes and remain absolutely still. This is very important because once you start to shuffle about or move any part of your relaxed self you totally disrupt the calm state and will have to begin again. Pause at each full stop.

JACK IN THE GREEN

Clearly imagine you are walking down a path leading through a field of meadow grass. Smell the cut hay. Feel the wind and warmth of the summer Sun upon your face. Look around and see brightly coloured wild flowers in the hedges which surround the field. Relax even more, and let all your senses appreciate the sights, smells, feelings and sounds of this country place.

Follow the well-trodden path across the meadow into the shadow of a copse of summer leafed trees. Sense the cooler air, hear the rustle of leaves, the chirp of birds. Smell the deep, leafy mould of the earth at your feet, and the sharper scent of the Sun upon the canopy of leaves. Reach out and touch the trunk of the nearest tree. Feel the roughness of the bark. Reach up and pull a springy twig so that you can see the leaves. Feel their texture. smoothness, curved edges. Smell them. Look at the twig examine its buds and the way the leaves join it. Let it go and hear the swish it makes.

Lean your back against the trunk of the tree and slide down until you are sitting among its roots. on the ground. Look up at the patterns the leaves and branches make. See sparkles of sunlight filtering down. Feel the strength and life of the tree.

Ask if it will talk with you. Wait for an answer, all the time relaxing and sinking deeper into the reality of the scene.

Notice who is coming towards you, through the trees nearby. It is Jack in the Green. He is a small man, wiry and bent with time. His hair is white like winter snow. His eyes are as blue as the skies of spring. His simple clothes are all the greens of the summer forest.

His wrinkled face, which smiles at you, is the brown of autumn beech leaves in the Sun. Somehow his clothes seem to be made of leaves, and there are trails of creeper about his neck and twined in his snowy beard– 'I have come to teach you,' *he says,* 'and I will take you to the Green Lady, when the moment is right.' *You know that he can tell you about the Wild Wood. You know he is kind and wise. You relax even more and find a question pops into your mind. You ask him, and wait whilst he considers and then tells you his answer. He sits beside you, yet not too close. You ask him two more questions, and wait while he finds an answer.*

You start to be aware that the time of this visit is ending. You may have made a little progress, and perhaps the questions you asked were not very important. The Green Man smiles again, and reaches inside his pocket. From it he brings out a token, just for you. It is something of the forest; perhaps a twig, a nut, a strange shaped knot of dry wood. It is your passport. Accept it gratefully and thank him. Thank him, too, for answering your questions, and assure him that you will return, for you wish to meet the Green Lady.

You rise to your feet, using the tree behind you to get up.

You turn to see which way Jack in the Green will go, but he has already vanished. You walk slowly back along the path to the meadow. You are still very aware of the scents, sounds, sights and feelings of the cool copse. Coming forth the sunlight dazzles you, and the warmth of the Sun beckons you. Slowly, still recalling every detail of what you heard and sensed, you allow the meadow to dissolve. Gradually, gently, you take a deep breath, stretch your arms and open your eyes. Taking your time, you refocus on the familiar room and its contents.

After every journey into the Otherworld, even such a basic one as this, it is important to do three things. The first is, always write a brief account of your adventure, your questions and any answers you received. Think about the token he gave you, which will not be visible in this waking world. If you feel at all strange, as well you might, have a snack and a warm drink, for that is the second important thing to do. The third thing is to allow the images and experiences to trickle over into your memory. It is worthwhile thinking back over each part of the experience and seeing how you were affected by anything in your ordinary world. For example, did noises intrude? Were you aware of your body? Did you manage to see clearly each part of the short walk, or was it vague? Did you only sense or 'imagine' what it might be like? These are aspects of your own subconscious which you will have to come to terms with. The inner realms are real, they have laws and scenery, activities and weather just as your everyday world has, but it is by being able to find a reality in the Otherworld that you will be able to work Wild Witchcraft.

Travel this road many times. Jack in the Green is an ancient traditional figure. He is a spirit of the Wild Wood and a younger son of Pan, God of the animal kingdom, although we usually see him as an old man. His face peers at you from churches; he has been carved on many old buildings as a reminder of our heritage of knowledge of plants, trees and herbs. He was a gardener and knows the uses of every wild plant, fruit, herb and flower, but you will need to check that you have clearly understood what he might show you or explain on later visits. You will have to study good, illustrated herbals and tree identification books if you are not sure what every plant you encounter might be. It is usually safest to begin with the conventional kitchen herbs, and to learn their properties – which extend far beyond flavouring food.

HERB AND PLANT LORE

Look in your garden or plant a window box with green and spearmint, thyme, rosemary, basil, chives, comfrey, feverfew, lemon balm, and all the rest. Many of these can be used in infusions or teas, as hair rinses, in baths to relax, calm or invigorate you. There are many very good books, which will tell you about the plants in your area or country. Examine the idea of making natural fruit wines, preserves, jellies and pickles – so long as you are not greedy and avoid picking rare or protected species – for these can be incorporated into festivals you may celebrate, marking the passing of the seasons. Carefully follow instructions about drying and keeping herbs. Many of the green ones can be picked and frozen, when they are at their best, to be used in the winter: others can be cultivated in small pots and kept in a greenhouse or indoors to be available most of the year.

If you can find an evening class or personal instruction in the use of herbs, that is far better than trying to fathom out what is what from a book, even those with coloured pictures. Many herbs are very alike, and some are like weeds or harmful plants, so do take care. The old herbalists and wise women grew up with the wild plants all round them, and they learned their uses and magical powers·from childhood. If you start as an adult to master this vast subject, you will need patience and care and a certainty that what you are doing is safe.

Plant materials have many other uses in natural magic. The scented woods of apple, pine, cherry and larch, cedar and sandalwood may be used as incenses; as may the gums and resins of fruit trees, and pine in particular. Dried stems of sweet herbs, lavender, rosemary, thyme and southernwood also burn sweetly on charcoal. Experiment, but be careful if you are using plants you do not know well. Some can have very strange effects.

It is not possible in a book this size even to begin to

teach all the ways in which wood, twigs, leaves, fruit, flowers, buds, roots and seeds may be used in magic. Much of the oldest knowledge of this sort has never even been written down, for it was secretly handed down within families and clans, whose speciality was plant lore. Intuition will guide you to know what may be used for healing, for bathing, for purifications, for medicines, for divinations and for spices and wines. Every plant and herb has a variety of uses, from its wood, bark, roots, leaves and flowers, to make dyes, remedies, foods, fibres, building and artistic materials, and things which are a pleasure to have around us. We must treat these ancient sources of all manner of valuable materials with respect. When we need a piece of wood, we must take care not to damage the tree; when we want fruit or flowers we should take only enough and not be greedy. We can spend days of careful searching among all the shrubs in our area before we actually cut a dowsing rod or wand from a hazel or almond tree. We should examine the hedgerows thoroughly before cutting a staff or a 'stang', to give an old country name to a fork-topped walking stick.

We must learn to treat Nature as a living force and not as a basic source of raw materials, to be hacked at without a second thought. The carefully chosen wand, or dowsing rod or staff will serve us for many years. It will give pleasure, direct our wills, expand our perceptions when seeking water or minerals.

To learn more about the uses of trees, branches, wood and plants, you will need to seek expert advice. Some of that can come from books, from friends, from experienced gardeners, woodworkers or herbalists. Also know that many real sources of wisdom can come from deep within us, if we are willing to trust the inherited sources and ancient memories we can gain access to. By venturing into those inner worlds in a relaxed but alert state, we can meet the Old Ones, Gods and Goddesses of times-past, Elemental Beings linked with the life of rocks and forests, of springs and fire. To go warily into these other realms, treating as friends those we encounter there, asking them for help, guidance and knowledge to supplement what we can gain by mundane enquiry, we will learn more of our natural heritage.

Returning along the path through the fields into the sacred grove, it is possible to go one stage further, but only when you have walked the first path many times. Sit down in your quiet room, place a notebook and pen handy, dim the lights and burn some incense or vaporise perfume if you find this helps you enter that poised inner state. Allow yourself a few minutes of deliberate relaxation, sinking within, breathing easily and deeply, closing your eyes and re-opening them inwardly to see clearly the inner landscape.

THE GREEN LADY

Sense the summer warmth, smell the earth and greenery, feel the breeze and the brush of the long grass about you. Walk slowly across the meadow until you enter the shade of the grove of sacred trees. Quietly call for Jack in the Green to leave his hidden den and come forth to guide you. Hold out the token he gave you, once again felt and seen in your hand. Listen to the trees and the voices of the birds, the hum of insects and the wind in the greenery. Be still and wait until Jack has come to meet you. Clearly express your wish to meet the Green Lady. Hear what he has to tell you, and be ready to do as he says. Follow him amid the tall trunks, the green undergrowth, the scented bushes and climbing vines. Tread quietly within the sacred grove, harming nothing by thought or action.

Notice how the light has dimmed and the trunks of trees crowd closer. See how their leaves make a dark green ceiling above you. Be aware of pale blossoms of sweet-scented honeysuckle, bright holly berries on their dark bushes, even in this summer time. Press forward, making a way between leafy boughs into a sheltered and secluded glade within. Here you notice bright shafts of sunlight which penetrate the shade, and within, although dimly at first, you see a seated figure. You cannot make out her face but your attention is caught by the many animals and birds which suddenly seem to be all round you. On a fallen tree sits a beautiful Lady, her face hidden by a mane of rich, golden hair. At her feet is a fawn, and rabbits, shy badgers, foxes and hares sit unafraid. You creep nearer and though many pairs of eyes turn towards you and the wild creatures stiffen, none of them flees. As you draw closer, you see that the Lady is dressed in a green cloak, and underneath she has a gown made up of patterns of flowers, dark at the hem and bright about her pale throat. You bow for you know she is a Goddess, the Earth Mother, Gaia.

She may well speak to you, asking what you wish. what you can offer in her service. how you can help her restore the Wasteland, both within the land and inside the people. Her voice is soft, accented with a country lilt, yet the eyes that look out at you from the mass of shining hair are those of an experienced and wise woman.

You sit at her feet, gazing up at her. You try to understand who she is, what she can do, how you can help. Time passes, in silence or quiet conversation. Suddenly there is the shrieking alarm call of a blackbird, and without a pause the wild creatures flee. Birds in the trees above take wing, crying their alarm calls too and when you look again, the Green Lady has gone, but in the glade at your feet lies a bright feather. You know it is another token and will help you to meet her again. She may teach you of her wisdom, and you may make a dedication to her service. She is the Mistress of Green Magic, she Is the Old One, Lady of the Wild, Mother Nature. And you, Child of Earth, are her child too.

Turn and quietly walk back the way you came, Jack will guide your steps until you have passed through the green wood, crossed the flowery meadow and returned safe to your own home. Slowly breathe, and open your eyes. Remember everything you have seen and heard.

———

CHAPTER THREE
THE SACRED WATERS

'Let the Salt of Earth admonish the Water to bear the virtue of the Great Sea. Mother, be thou adored.'
MAGIC, IN THEORY AND PRACTICE – Aleister Crowley

The ancient peoples in many lands divided all that they could see into four or five elements, those most commonly used in the West being Earth, Water, Fire and Air. There is a fifth element, Spirit or Aether, which is the quintessence of the others, but in the simpler arts of natural magic, the original four are enough to deal with. Each has a valid part to play in the lives of everyone, both ancient and modern. True, we do not now depend so heavily on fire for heating, lighting and cooking, yet we still require electrical energy which is always produced by fire in one way or another, either burning coal or oil, or the heat of a nuclear reaction.

We need air to breathe, as does every living creature, plant and fish, and the Earth beneath our feet not only maintains a platform to live on as we travel through space, but it also provides the raw materials from which, ultimately, come all our foods, houses, clothing and every material thing we possess.

———

THE SACRED WATERS

Water too is vital to all living beings in one form or another, and its lack when the rains fail, perhaps destroys more life than anything else in Nature. We too are largely made up of water; flowing in our blood, lubricating our joints, in our tears, saliva and glandular secretions. Because we are watery beings, we are also to a minor degree tidal, like any ocean. The effect the Moon has upon the waters of the Earth is in some small way reflected in our moods and emotions, for Water is the element which rules these innermost feelings. Anyone who lives near the sea, or a tidal stretch of river or estuary, will always inwardly know the state of the tide and feel in their own bones the ebb and flow of the great oceans. Inland folk will still often experience times of calm and periods of restlessness, which reflect these vast forces of the external world working upon us.

As the gravity of the Moon raises and lowers the tides of the sea each day, so her position and her waxing and waning power also affect us, particularly at those levels of our inner life over which we have no conscious control. The patterns of our dreams are Moon led, and the peaks and troughs of our emotions can often be determined by the phase of the Moon. It is acknowledged in some hospitals that mental patients are more disturbed at the Full Moon and in surgical wards patients may bleed more at this time. Suicides occur statistically more frequently at the time of the Full Moon too, so we should become aware of how powerful the effect on us can be of this ignored satellite of Earth. Try to discover how you are affected by this tide ruler in the heavens above.

SACRED SPRINGS

All kinds of water sources have been sacred in the past and many of the ancient civilizations believed that life arose from the seas, even as scientists now consider that evolution did begin in water. Rivers and pools, springs and hot spa waters have always been considered places of healing, magic or blessing. In Britain and much of Europe, every freshwater spring was originally thought to be under the care of a Guardian or Water Nymph. In later times these ancient keepers became known as saints in many places.

Look at any map and trace the village names. Every town, hamlet or dwelling had to have a source of drinking water for the people and livestock. The earliest cities sprang up on river banks or around freshwater lakes. Place names often derive from watery links: spring, bourne, pool, puddle, venton (Cornish for fountain), mere, burn, brook, purl and, of course, actual river names: Kingston-upon-Thames, Stockton-on-Tees or Upton-on-Severn. There are probably dozens in all languages, from Aquae Sulis, the Latin name for Bath, through Celtic Avondale and all kinds of Saxon and Norman French words so unnoticeably incorporated in the words we see around us all the time.

Most of the old communities' wells or springs were

thought of as holy or sacred. They were nearly always under the care of a Goddess – in Celtic legend she was Bride, Brid or, in Christian connotation, St Brigit. There are to this day many hundreds of holy wells still bringing forth clear water. Some are well-known, like Malvern water which is drunk as a matter of course by many people as an alternative to tap water. The number of spa water sources in Britain is growing all the time, with pure or medical springs being exploited by those who have a preference for water as Nature intended – not the recycled, chlorinated and chemically treated stuff that comes out of our taps! Many people are making use of water filters to get rid of the artificial taste and the hardness which furs up kettles and pipes. The authorities have a tough job preventing nitrates seeping from farm fertilizers into drinking water and other chemicals polluting streams from which many households actually draw their water via filter beds and simple purification plants.

We all take it for granted that the water is safe to drink, that there is any amount of it, for bathing, washing clothes and cleaning the house, yet in many parts of the world water is a scarce commodity and its purity is doubtful. Like other resources, we must try not to waste this natural product, not only by taking care when we are actually using it, but also by ensuring we do not have leaking pipes or dripping taps in our homes, as over the months these can allow many gallons to trickle away.

Not only are the sources of water considered holy, but water itself has been used to cleanse and bless things in many religions and in many folk cults too. Roman Catholics are familiar with the sprinkling of Holy water in the Mass and the baptism of babies or young people; other religions also involve washing, something which strict Muslims do each time they pray, five times a day. In India bathing in Mother Ganges river is thought to purify and bless those who perform this rite.

In many branches of the Christian religion, the baptism of children by sprinkling with water and adults by total immersion, is used both to purify the individual – washing away sin – and to dedicate him to a new life in Christ. Often it is used as part of the Christening ceremony when a baby is named. Chrism is the Greek word for oil, so one who has been anointed with oil becomes a christ! Many Eastern festivals involve the sprinkling of water, often over the whole congregation, for it magically helps the rains to appear in times of drought. The Native Americans have rain dances and even Morris Men dance to change the weather, leaping high and waving white hankies which represent the clouds passing by.

CONSECRATION
Water is not only used to cleanse churches, it is often used in a variety of ways in pagan ceremonies. In this case rock salt is added, as described at the head of this chapter

in the quote from the Gnostic Mass. Earth, in the form of rock salt (other salt is taken out of the sea, so it is watery already), is mixed with water and this is used to bless the priest of that ritual. In modern witch ceremonies, water is blessed in a similar way and is sprinkled around the circle to make it a sacred place for the duration of the ritual. Often water used to be simply blessed by the acting priest or priestess and then it was shaken over the congregation or other participants from a sprig of a sacred or magical herb like rue or rosemary, rowan or bay. It is one of the first magical acts of consecration that anyone might wish to learn, for it is by blessing things with holy water that they are changed and made sacred. To bless some water, take a bowl and half fill it with spring water (bottled will do), or rain water, which is better than tap water unless you intend to drink it. Take a deep breath and pointing the first two fingers of your right hand at the water say:

'Lady of the Living Waters, bless this thy symbol, driving from it all impurities, that it may become a pure and sacred source of power. So mote it be.'

The water may then be used to bless other things over which it is sprinkled, using a similar formula:

'Lady (or Lord) of ... bless this creature of ... purify it and instill in it your magical power. So mote it be.'

When the thing has been cleansed and blessed with water, you may use a similar prayer calling upon the Lord of Fire, the Lady of Earth and the Lord of Air, to consecrate a candle for Fire, some salt or earth for Earth, and incense, the smoke of which represents Air.

If you have a training in the use of other God and Goddess names or you wish to use the Archangels, then that will work just as well. The names you should never use are those you do not understand. It is all very well copying words or rituals from some book, but unless you actually know what it is that you are calling upon, you have no idea what sort of response you will get. This is important; so if you are thinking of using prayers, rituals or any kind of magical spell involving words you have not chosen yourself, you must understand them exactly or you could be asking for trouble.

For this reason it is always much safer simply to say 'Lady of Water', 'Lord of Fire', 'Spirit of Healing', or whatever you really need, so that there is no confusion in your mind and no muddle when some ancient power is called forth to do some task which is not in its normal repertoire. Even if you think you know what the names mean, or they are Celtic or local names, unless you are absolutely certain of what you are calling upon, it is better to make up a phrase which exactly fits the bill. Most of the classical God and Goddess names are titles, or 'job descriptions' in modern terms. So what seems like a good idea at the time, can have you calling upon a Goddess who is a large pig and famed for destroying her children, rather than the nice Moon Maiden that you thought she was!

———

CONSECRATION OF SELF

You may use water to cleanse and bless yourself in a variety of ways and for several different purposes. The first is fairly obvious, that of ritual bathing. One of the easiest and safest ways of making good use of herbs, apart from cooking with them, is to use them in a bath. A few sprigs of lemon balm, rosemary, lavender or mint, tied in thin muslin and hung where the hot water can run through it, will ensure that you emerge not only cleaner but refreshed or relaxed, depending upon your choice of herb. If you bruise the leaves and stems a little first, you will get the benefit of the scent as well as some of the essential oils which make these plants so fragrant. If you cannot set aside time from the family or other commitments, a meditational bath can often serve a useful purpose. Some people manage to use scents in the bathroom even when the others in their household object to the smell of proper incenses, and a bath by candlelight can make it all the more magical.

You may bless yourself with consecrated water at the beginning of a meditation or inner journey, for this is a way of telling your inner self that you are doing something special. A bowl of water is blessed with similar words to those just described, or with words of your own choosing. Again, do not use God or Goddess names unless you are certain that they are appropriate. You can sprinkle a little water from your fingers, or a twig over your head, saying:

'Lady, bless me, and gently open the pathways of my understanding, that when I enter the inner realms I need not fear, and that those I encounter there will offer help and security. So mote it be.'

You may use any words you prefer, of course: this is just a guide to the sort of thing to say. It is always far safer and more effective to make up your own sets of prayers, blessings, consecrations and other special words because your intention is always different to anyone else's, so their words may not be exactly right. Like all magical arts, making up these short invocations comes with practice, as do the other techniques of meditation and inner journeys.

... AND PLACE OF WORK

You may also bless the circle around you, sprinkling water clockwise at the start of your work and anti-clockwise at the end to wind down the power and complete the job in hand. This winding down is a very important aspect of all magical work, for otherwise, you are leaving doors to your psyche – the sensitive part of your subconscious mind – wide open, so that you can be influenced by anything around you. On the mundane level this could just mean becoming susceptible to advertising and buying things you do not need. On a deeper level, you may pick up other people's thoughts, doubts, despairs and miseries, to which you would normally be impervious.

If you are not able actually to walk in circles around your meditation chair, you can sprinkle the water to the four quarters of the compass – East, South, West and North in turn – and imagine either a Guardian Angel standing there or one of the mighty Elemental Beings of that element. These are very real so do not ignore them and walk through them, or forget to thank them at the end of anything you do. Just because you may not see them at the beginning of your studies does not mean they have not offered you the protection and calmness you asked for! Always in magical work, be polite, responsible and earn respect from those you deal with. That is how true magical power is built: by co-operating with, rather than commanding to do your bidding, beings who are much bigger, older and wiser than you are.

When you start to collect a set of magical equipment – like bowls to place symbols of the four elements in – you will need to cleanse and then dedicate each object separately to its magical future. This same type of consecration should be applied to your meditation robe, any kinds of special altar cloths, crystal balls or scrying mirrors, tarot cards and so on. Each thing then becomes special and must be kept apart, ideally in a locked cupboard or box, so that prying eyes and hands do not undo your ritual of consecration. It is tempting to show all your friends your special robe and magical items because you think this will help convince them of the validity of your studies, but the opposite is nearly always

———

true. If they thought you were strange before, then if you give them a fashion show of your robe, exhibit your water and incense, bowls and the special rock you use as a symbol of the earth, they will think even less of you and all the magic which may have been built up about those objects will vanish. You will then have to learn the hard lesson of secrecy and discretion and start from the beginning again, re-consecrating and blessing every object, and yourself.

Secrecy and discretion do matter. If you keep quiet about your studies, put away your meditation robe, diary and any things which you have collected to help you with your work, these things will all build up a strong aura of magic about them. This, in turn, will help you to change to that level of inner perception. Your meditations and inner journeys will be clearer and your spells and workings more effective.

Most people long for others to share their work, their rituals and cycles of celebrations. Others will come, especially if you ask the Lady and the Lord to guide you to meet them. You will need to take steps to discover other folk on the same path, however, and not just sit by the front door, waiting for a witch or an adept to turn up at your request! Go to the library and ask about local clubs, leave discreet messages on health food shop notice-boards, hover in the bookshops where occult books are sold and see who you meet. Look in the national magazines on magical subjects to see about societies, lectures, groups or festivals where you might meet suitable folk. Before you go to such gatherings, always ask to be protected from anyone who might wish you harm and that you will encounter those people who can be most helpful to you. Afterwards, have a magical bath to wash off any strange energies you might have picked up, and give thanks for the seeds of future friendships that may have been sown. You do not often get immediate results, so do be patient, and use your common sense, especially if someone offers you initiation or admittance to anything on first meeting you!

You may be able to serve the Old Gods by finding out where your nearest spring is. Even in cities there are Holywell Roads or Spring Gardens and the like. An old Ordnance Survey map will show springs, wells and small streams for your area. Again, the local reference library will have such maps for you to look at, and probably dozens of funny, old-fashioned guidebooks describing many features that are no longer visible – like horsetroughs where the dray and cab horses drank, each filled from a spring or runnel. If your house was built before about 1830 it may have had its own well or spring or there would have been one in the area, perhaps shared by a hamlet. Again, old maps will tell you all about this forgotten aspect of our land's history. The names of fields, copses, old houses and farms will often give clues too, so find out some of the words which relate to pagan or magical sites.

———

DOWSING

It is worth mastering the old art of dowsing, too. This can be done with a hazel or willow twig in the shape of the letter 'Y', about as long as your forearm and with the outer part as thick as your thumb. Do not hack the hazel or willow trees about. Get yourself a pair of sharp secateurs especially for cutting wands or pruning shrubs and make a clean and neat job. They are far kinder to the trees than hacking away with a magical knife, especially if it is ceremonially blunt as most of them tend to be! Search hard and only cut one wand or rod at a time.

When you have it, carefully trim any side branches and make sure that the ends of the 'Y' are smooth because you hold these. To use the traditional grip, place both hands with the palms up, thumbs facing out, in a sort of offering position. Now balance the rod across your hands, with the short arm of the 'Y' pointing forward and the ends of the longer arms across the bases of your fingers and sticking through the gap below your first finger and thumb. Gently close your fingers so that the rod bends a bit wider and your elbows dig into your ribs. The short part should now point upwards. When you walk about in this position, while concentrating on the idea of water, you will usually find after a few goes that, as you cross a stream or underground water pipe, the tip of the rod turns sharply downwards, twisting within your hands. It does take a certain knack to do it, but with practice at least nine out of ten people can get it to work if they persevere. There are many good books on dowsing.

Pendulums can also be used to detect energy fields round people, places and objects. Once you have found a suitable small weight – a heavy bead or a chipped marble, for example, stuck with epoxy resin to the end of a couple of handspans of thin picture cord (the end of the cord should be frizzled with a match and slapped down on a hard surface, to provide a flat end to stick to the marble), you simply need to establish a personal code for 'yes' and 'no', or positive and negative. Ask a question with an obvious 'yes' answer, for example, 'Is grass green?' The pendulum's reaction is your 'yes' code. Repeat for 'no', for example, 'Is grass purple?' The pendulum can swing in left and right-handed circles, back and forth, or side to side, in respect of your body. With practice, in normal circumstances you will have an established inner code – one movement for 'yes' and another for 'no'. This may alter if you are asking questions for or about someone else, so do check, especially if you are using the pendulum to find a cure for an illness or the seat of a problem.

Once you have found your initial code and assured yourself that it is stable and the pendulum responsive, you can search for missing objects. See if you can detect which of two similar magical items has been consecrated and which has not. You can use your other hand for pointing, to find the edges of fields of energy around things and, with a willing friend, you can test their energy centres, or chakras, to see if they are all functioning in harmony. The wider the swing, the more energy there is; the more balanced the set, the healthier the individual.

You may use a pendulum over the food you eat, testing each item in turn to see if any of them are specially good for you, or whether some are actually harmful or cause allergic reactions. This can often surprise you, and you can test the reliability of this method by ceasing to eat those harmful things for a week or two and seeing how you feel. You can also test substances around you – like chemicals, medicines or household products – using Nature's special sense to see what is good and what is bad, for her and for you.

Out of doors you can detect underground pipes for water, gas or electricity (if you keep your mind on what you are looking for), and you may detect minerals, rocks or natural energy sources in the gardens or fields that you visit. You can watch animals 'dowsing', for when they lie down, even humble sheep and cows choose the spot with care, to energize or rest themselves according to Nature's energy flows. Dogs and cats do it too, if they are given a chance, selecting interesting and varied spots around the house depending on their current mood. Try dowsing in the same place and see if you can discover what it is that they like. It may not be as obvious as heat or cold! Ask mental questions and allow the pendulum to give its opinion. The pendulums and dowsing rods work because we all have the ability to detect various energy fields, but this knowledge is supplied at too weak a level for most of us to detect without some kind of instrument or amplifier, which the rod or pendulum basically is.

This is a very ancient skill, mostly overlooked, yet taking only a very short time to master. Like meditation, entering the Otherworld through inner journeys, or developing the ability to sense the pain or needs of other people, this dowsing ability is simple. That does not, however, mean that it is easy.

The hardest thing about relearning these arts and crafts is accepting that you basically have the talent or knack to do them. The one thing that prevents most people making use of their inherent skills is the word 'can't'. I have been teaching various magical methods for many years, and many people say, 'but I can't meditate' or, 'I can't read tarot cards'. What they are muddling up is the knowledge and the practice. They may not yet know how to meditate or to make something of the tarot, but it is not impossible for them to do these things once they have been instructed and have tried them out. It is best to substitute the word 'can't' with 'will try': 'I will try to meditate ...' Or it is often easier just to add the word 'yet' as in, 'I can't read the tarot cards yet ...'

Dowsing is a perfect example of this non-acceptance of a future ability. Once you have made a pendulum, wound it round your fingers so that it dangles a handspan below them and allowed it to swing and move in command of your inner mind, you have a very useful indicator always at your bidding. You can test herbal or other natural medicines, and if you study any of the variety of healing arts, you can often use the pendulum to confirm your diagnosis or your suggestions to help the sick person.

It is well worth getting some proper training in any of the modern versions of old healing methods because then you have two approaches. You do need confidence in your ability, and that will only come with regular use and practice, so that eventually you can do it without having to use a rod or pendulum to interpret your feelings at the site of water, or identify the direction to go when something is lost, or even locate faults in your car.

HEALING SPAS

Although they are not as popular now as they were in Britain in the 18th century, there are quite a number of spa towns in the countryside, or places where springs or wells are known for their healing power. This traditional form of healing is still extremely popular in Europe, especially in France, Germany and Italy. In these countries, people may receive spa treatment as part of their National Health Service if they have the kind of conditions which mineral water baths will heal.

In Russia and Iceland there are hot springs which are

very popular with people suffering from stiff joints and rheumatic complaints, and in Japan therapy involving the use of ice packs on swollen joints is being found very effective. In each case water is the healing agent.

Most of the British spas are now just tourist places. The hot springs at Bath in the West Country, for example, are not available for healing at the present time for the general public at all. Tunbridge Wells spa seems to have degenerated into a soft drinks bar, although that particular inky tasting spa water does need something to make it palatable in large quantities. Buxton Spa, Leamington and Cheltenham all seem to have fallen out of favour in the natural healing field, yet each month there seem to be more articles in the media on traditional or alternative forms of therapy. Spas did not arise as the whim of some money-making individual. They were known in the 18th century to the local folk who used the waters to heal themselves and their livestock long before their rise to fame. Glastonbury was also made into a spa town but the water from the mystical Chalice Well is very cold, and it is generally the magical rather than the healing properties which draw people to that special place at present.

THE ART OF SCRYING

Perhaps the time has come for those on the magical paths to reinvoke the healing and occult powers of these ancient and sacred watering places. Water is not only the source of physical healing but can be used to bring comfort and wisdom to the focused mind – for many a deep pool or slow running stream was also a place of oracular vision. The priestesses in most of the world's oldest temples were trained to use the magical powers of water for scrying. Usually after a ritual bath they were taken to a place where still dark water was to be seen and there, using it as we might gaze at a glass ball or mirror, they were able to descry things which were happening far away or long ago. Certainly some woodland streams running over dark pebbles or peaty pools on the moor have a hypnotic and magical air to them, and it is not difficult to use them to help you switch into a receptive mode. Be careful, though, for you can become so drawn to the water that you fall in, head first!

Indoors, it is possible to use a glass bowl full of spring water for scrying. This is a lot easier for beginners than the use of a glass or crystal ball, especially if the carefully cleaned and polished bowl is placed on a black cloth before you start to scry. Dim the lights, light a stick of incense, relax and gaze steadily into the water. Ask the Spirit of Water to teach you, show you her magical visions, and allow time for your inner sight to clear. Be patient, this is one of the more difficult sorts of basic magic, for it requires a poised state of mind.

After a while, you will start to see changes in the water, mist or a dimming of the surface, and then ... who knows? Often shapes, colours, images and eventually fully formed three-dimensional moving pictures will emerge from the centre of the swirling mist and flow outwards to fill all your vision. It seldom happens first time off, but if you have spent some time becoming familiar with the techniques of meditation and inner journeying, then you will be halfway there and results will come more quickly and clearly.

When you have finished, even if your efforts were not very rewarding, always say a polite 'thank you' to the Spirit of Water, and pour the water on to the Earth. If you learn to consecrate the water first – though for scrying salt is best left out – and always act politely to anyone you have asked for help and guidance, you will gradually get better at each art.

You can actually make really magical 'scrying water' by exposing a glass bowl to the light of the waning Moon. When the Moon is full, place a dish on a window sill so that the moonlight is reflected in it. Call upon the Lady of the Moon, who is also the teacher of many psychic arts, to bless and consecrate the water so that it might become a clear vehicle for scrying, and so that your own abilities will be increased during the next waxing phase. The waning light will take wisdom and knowledge inwards to the deeper levels of inner sight, and the waxing light will bring forth those newly gained abilities into consciousness. Keep your Moon-blessed water separately in a bottle in a dark place so that it does not get polluted. You can also add a little of it to your bath water for magical bathing, or use it to bless yourself and if the water was pure and has been kept clean, you can drink it as a further link with your psychic self, awakened by the Moon's power.

It is an old ritual to go out and look at the Moon's face reflected in a pool or puddle, watching strange impressions flit across your awareness as the clouds shape her circle or the ripples of the wind shift and multiply her reflection. You can learn the true art of Drawing Down the Moon, not with daggers indoors, but into water or by reflected mirror-light into magical wine. Here, the Moon's own power is drawn into a liquid, instead of as in the witch Priestess' ritual where the Goddess power is drawn into the High Priestess. There are strange powers in Moonlight, which are not obvious in the light of day or in the minds of those who will not acknowledge them.

The Old Ones knew how best to use these secret and subtle powers but we have to learn them anew, step by step, at dark and new and Full Moon phases, with sacred water and with dark wine. Ask the Goddess, she will teach you.

CHAPTER FOUR

THE FLAME AND THE FORM

*'I am the flame that burns in the heart of every man, and in the
core of every star. I am life, and the giver of Life, yet therefore is
the knowledge of me the knowledge of death. I am alone;
there is no God where I am...'*

MAGIC, IN THEORY AND PRACTICE – Aleister Crowley

Although natural magic is essentially simple, we
have become quite complicated people, so the
methods modern practitioners use differ from those of
our ancestors in many ways.

Most of the inner aspects of magic cannot be written
down because they are experiential. If you are not
willing to experiment and learn from what happens
in each case, you will never master magic. Every piece
of occult work is a leap into the dark. Every spell you
utter, every talisman you make is an experiment, and
the results will depend entirely upon your sincerity and
dedication, rather than your knowledge or expertise.

Generally, we learn things at school. However,
this overlooks the fact that much of what we need to
know is very different from the reading, writing and
arithmetic taught in ordinary schools – especially when

you get into the realms of the other worlds, and mental and psychic skills. These are rarely even considered to be real, let alone as a basis for school lessons. Yet such basic abilities as those of meditation, creative vision and self-confidence brought about by knowing that you have practical knowledge and wisdom from your own resources, are often far more useful in real life than algebra or sociology.

Those who seek to tread the magical paths will soon recognise that you can never cease learning; not only by adding new ideas but also by looking again at bits of earlier knowledge and seeing these in much greater depth. As each day passes, new things happen to us and new knowledge is gained. That was the way the old folk magicians gained their abilities to heal, see into the future and manage all the small rituals and spells which they needed to help themselves or those around them. None of them had the chance to study a course of instruction, or even read books of magical learning. They would make use of the things about them and by expanding their awareness beyond the here and now, would be able to observe future trends, discover lost animals or make protective charms as was necessary.

We live in a world in which everything is categorized and set apart from everything else. Yet the truth of the matter is that nothing is separate. Every individual person is linked genetically to his or her family and each one is part of the Earth in as much as their food and drink is taken from the fruits and vegetables growing on the Earth. We are subject to the weather, the seasons, time and experience, as every other living thing is, and this gives us the link with other beings through which magic can work. It is the understanding of the specific links between things that forms a large part of the basis of modern magic.

In earlier times, objects and even people's natures were classified under the four elements. Such terms as 'down to earth', a 'fiery temper', 'airy-fairy ideas' or plain 'wet', are still in common usage today although we seldom realize what we are saying when we apply them. One of the most useful systems, applicable both to natural magic and to the more formal ceremonial or Qabalistic traditions, is that of correspondences. This is a system of lists whereby all sorts of things are classified and so linked, perhaps with the four elements, or the seven planets of the old astrologers, or the twelve Signs of the Zodiac. This is a useful way of associating various items which might be used to make a talisman, for example.

UNDERLYING PRINCIPLES

As magic works by conforming with several underlying principles, it is important to have a rough idea of what these principles are. Some of the oldest evidence for the use of magic is shown where Stone Age painters have depicted on their cave ceilings, a shaman or hunter disguised in the skin and antlers of a stag. It is usually quoted as a demonstration of 'sympathetic magic', in that the magician acts out the successful hunt so that when they go after real deer the hunters of the tribe will bring home the meat.

This form of play-acting appears to be a very old and powerful form of magic. There are other factors which are worth considering too. One of them is that of 'Thanksgiving', for by taking the part of the stag, the shaman is acknowledging the power of the animal's spirit, and by his ritual act of appeasement he is symbolically asking that when that deer has been caught, another will take its place in some future hunt. Even to this day, the Inuit still make some gesture to appease the angry spirits of the fish or seals they hunt for meat, so that the spirit can be reborn as another animal.

Another aspect of the work of the shaman priest was that of tracking down something to hunt. This would have implied, very early in humanity's history, an ability to see beyond the horizon; not only of place, but of time, for most of the herds upon which the people depended for food were grazing, and thus roaming, animals. They could not be expected to stay in one place for very long, especially if they had been frightened by the approach of hunters. Ripe fruit, roots or berries would also have to be found, as well as sources of water in the drier landscapes where early humanity grew up. It is most likely that even the first clans or family groups recognised the inherited skill of a man or woman who could guess correctly where such supplies were to be found. Modern magicians and witches cultivate the same ability even if they are shopping in a supermarket or visiting a street market. Knowing where the best, the cheapest and the freshest fruit and vegetables are is just as important now, even though we can look it up on our mobile device!

OF FIRE AND FLAME

One of the sources of such knowledge must have lain deep within the consciousness of our ancient ancestors, just as it remains largely buried within our modern minds. We use similar methods to bring such intuitions to the surface to this day – we gaze at water or at the shimmering flame of a small candle. After the Wood Age, humanity must have turned its developing technological know-how to the subject of fire. Created in heaven, bursting forth from the sky as lightning, setting fire to trees or dry grasses – it must have been seen as a gift from the sky God. Many ancient people have legends as to how heroes such as the Greek Prometheus brought fire for the use of the people. The Maoris have similar tales, as do the Australian Aborigines, where a bird or animal helped the early people steal this valuable asset from the Gods.

Fire provided heat in winter and light for those secret magical places deep within the rocky caves where the most elaborate burial sites and the most potent magical

---

paintings on the rocks are to be found, in Europe and Australia, in America and South Africa. Everywhere that the Earth made special places deep inside her rocky mantle, there the shamans would go, taking small lamps and whole ranges of natural colours with which to paint the sacred hunt, pictures of the people, and especially images of the animals from which they derived their livelihood. Only the medium of fire would allow them to work in the dark, and the flickering flames would reanimate the spirit pictures so that the dead seemed to live again. That basic technology is still with us, although our homes are now mostly lit by electricity and living flames have been banished from both fireplace and lamp.

Magical work is nearly always carried out in the dim gleam of living flames: candles, nightlights, oil lamps, or sometimes just by the fire's glow if there is a working hearth, for here, another older reality makes itself manifest. Pictures can be seen in the glowing embers and bright flames, the dark coals, the grey ashes and burning wood, each offering another dimension which can so easily transport the trained watcher through the Gate of Fire into the Otherworld beyond. Such a form of clairvoyance is very ancient. In every temple and secret grove there was always a fireplace where offerings of sweet-smelling wood were burned, and where the 'Sacred fires were never allowed to whiten into ash', to quote a Roman writer describing the Sanctuary of Sulis Minerva at Bath.

These fires consumed the offerings of perfume, meat or incenses; they also provided a hearth into which the fire scryer could look to discover the intentions of the oracle. The woods used on these magical hearths were nearly always sacred in their own right, being small twigs from particular trees or even the stems of herbs like rosemary, dittany, sage, thyme or rue, and valerian – the temple herb – bringing both healing and vision. Of course people have recognised the strange effects certain burning plants have on their consciousness, not always to their own benefit, for anything which detracts from the user's control should never be used in magic today.

Oil lamps were used all over the classical world, burning mainly olive oil, but in chilly Britain the invading Romans and others had to make do with tallow dips – thin peeled rushes dipped into melted sheep's fat. Candles made of beeswax were very expensive and usually only burned on church altars at high festivals. Modern paraffin wax, which is used for the vast majority of commercial candles, is an off shoot of the petrochemical industry and so probably only a hundred years or so old. Simple lamps which burned any kind of animal fat were used to light, and to a certain extent heat, the homes of most of the poorer folk up until the introduction of coal gas and later electric light. We are used to the daylight brightness of neon tubes or electric bulbs, but it is really quite a new phenomenon. Most of

---

the modern magicians still use lamps and candles with real flames to light their ceremonies, to burn as offerings or magical omen bringers or to add a touch of living flame to a modern setting.

There is definitely a change of atmosphere brought about by turning off a light and using natural flames instead. It does make the most ordinary room seem magical and it produces that feeling of anticipation or excitement so vital to the success of any magical act. Like all the other things which are done to make the magician more effective, changing into a special robe and lighting incense, for example, dimming the light to the glow of a candle's flickering flame, can help to awaken those inner levels of perception which make divinations come clear or inner journeys more vivid. This may be explained as 'psychological effects', but that is where most of the changes to the world must begin. The low light, symbols, shapes, colours and feelings take on a new significance. New depths of perception come to the surface and any work done by candlelight will affect the innermost levels of awareness.

LEVELS OF AWARENESS

Nearly all magical work involves using several levels of perception. We are liable to forget that we need, in fact, to gain greater awareness, whatever our esoteric task might happen to be. Although for the duration of the task at hand, it is necessary to be less aware of the outside world, whilst we sit still to meditate or perform a simple ritual, we actually need a greater awareness to ensure that we gain every nuance of what is to be perceived during that time.

Our first level of awareness is that of the ordinary world about us. It is true that many people are so unaware of what is going on about them that if you ask what number bus just went by or even where to get some ordinary item from a shop, they do not have a clue what to tell you.

We are very liable to go through life in a kind of half dream, unless we make a conscious effort not to do so. In many of the Eastern philosophies you will find, time and time again such phrases as, 'we must wake up', 'we must gain awareness' or 'the purpose of stillness is to become alive'. At first sight, these often appear not to make much sense. Each one, however, is true. We will act almost entirely automatically unless we do something about it. We get up each day, wash, dress, even eat breakfast without focusing at all on what we are actually doing. Often this non-awareness flows over into the dull tasks of an ordinary day, at work, shopping, caring for the family, cooking and finally slumped in front of the television. To be a real magician, especially one who is working with Nature, means we have to be the exact opposite to that. We must live every waking and sleeping moment with full awareness.

To begin with it is necessary to train yourself. Think

------

which shoe you put on first, realize how much of an unconscious pattern your daily activities are and how little you notice of the world about you. All that must change. Perhaps to start with, it will help to give a kind of silent, running commentary to yourself about your actions, 'I am getting out of bed, my right foot is touching the cooler carpet, now I am walking to the bathroom, it is lighter here. The water makes a pleasant trickling noise, it is warm, the towel is rough ...' See how long you can keep this up. It is surprisingly difficult. Few people can concentrate for more than about fifteen minutes; for most it is far less than that. To work effective magic, you need an attention span of at least an hour or two!

You will not only need to concentrate on the visual things, for example, the furniture or the colour of the walls, but you will also need to focus on the feel of the clothes you are wearing, their weight, texture and comfort. You will need to listen to all the sounds, not only the obvious background music of our lives but also the rustle of cloth as you move and the thud of your pulse when there is silence outside. You will need to recognise distant bird song, a dog barking, the wind in the trees – yes, even in cities many of these sounds can be heard and identified.

You need to see much more, describing to yourself what it is that you are seeing and sensing: colour, depth, distance, light and shade. Become aware of scents: pleasant perfumes, sharp cooking smells, flowers, concrete, metals and textiles about you. Nature gave us all many senses, most of which we do not use. To benefit from her gifts and instruction we must stretch each of these to the limit, becoming very sensitive, and yet being able to switch off that sensitivity when it is not required. Only by continually becoming totally aware of what is going on all around us in ordinary circumstances are we able to glean information on other levels. Unless we know what is ordinary, we cannot recognise the messages from the inner which are extraordinary!

Learn to be still and listen not only to your body and the data coming in from your five senses, but listen to your mind. See if you can discover where thoughts and inspiration come from. Where in your being is your consciousness? Is it in your head, your heart, or even outside what most people would consider their physical body? Listen to your consciousness, and learn to listen to your heart and its feelings. Each is a separate channel of teaching and guidance. We ignore these as if they were not there, simply because we have not become aware of the important messages they can convey to our awareness in subtle ways.

Hear what your body has to say about its state of health, its needs for food, rest, exercise or cleansing. Treat it well, for it is a gift of the Goddess of Earth. Learn to love yourself by getting to know your body. You can improve its shape or weight, if you want to, it is your responsibility. It will serve you well for about eighty years if you care for it properly. Your body is an outer shell, loaned to you for the duration of one life, and if you are sensible it will stay healthy, warding off unpleasant illnesses, steering clear of cancer, heart diseases or lung troubles (if you ensure it is not polluted with smoking, as no sensible person smokes, especially any real magician!). Ensure your body has a balanced diet, vegetarian or not, according to your own choice as long as it is thought about and chosen consciously. Health is your choice, so overcome bad habits, love your physical self and learn to know and love your spirit too.

Seek to become aware of those inner levels of your being, your heart which rules your feelings, and your spirit which is eternal. Your feelings should be examined and not repressed.

Everyone feels angry, hurt or disappointed at times. At other times, the opposite is true. Love has to be gained by becoming lovable – even Jesus said, 'Love thy neighbour as thyself'! If you do not love yourself you cannot expect anyone else to love you. Give out feelings of hope, love, charity and goodness and these will be returned to you threefold, according to magical law. Smile and be polite to the real people that you deal with every day, and they will instantly, and seemingly magically, reward you with their full attention, with small acts of kindness or simply with a smile of recognition in return. A kind word will go a long way to gaining assistance, co-operation and respect from other people. That in turn oils the wheels of life.

On the inner levels if you are rude, demanding or imagine you have any right to command those beings who live there, you will be in for some very unpleasant surprises. On the inner you are the stranger, the uninvited guest, and if you do not behave well you will get little help – not because there is necessarily evil to be found there, but because your attitude will be exactly reflected back to you.

Awareness may seem to be an ethereal matter, but it is nevertheless a real fact of life. If you are unaware, no amount of magical spells, conjuring spirits or performing elaborate rituals will gain you an inch on your journey through life. Once you become aware, you clearly see the answers to your prayers, almost as fast as they are said. Divinations will very soon appear clear and lucid, healings will occur almost miraculously, simply because you perceive their happening. You will gain in ordinary life, for your whole existence will take on a new and more definite meaning. Whatever you do, whomever you meet, you will always be able to understand exactly what is going on.

The world will be a better place, for you will gradually be able to take control of every aspect of the things you do, not only on the magical levels, but in ordinary things too. You will see the patterns, recognize the energy flows which the world ignores, and by knowing whether these are running for or against your plans, you will be able to make the best use of them to achieve your objectives.

———

They cannot simply be explained, for every individual perceives them in a different way. Only knowing about them and then recognising them in your own terms will do.

As well as seeing what is going on all around you, it will be necessary to build up your knowledge and understanding of the symbols of the inner levels. These may be obvious, like learning the meanings of the 78 tarot cards or the 64 hexagrams of the *I Ching*, for example. It may well mean that you start to build up copies of the fourfold, sevenfold and twelve fold tables, of the elements, the planets and the Signs of the Zodiac. You will need to draw up a table and gradually collect the 'sets' of information under each heading. As an example, you can very quickly fill up the elements table by entering what you think the instrument of magic is for Earth, Water, Fire and Air. Then you can go on to which plants relate to each, which direction of the compass, which tarot suite, which colour, shape, symbol, incense, Elemental Being and so on. Make sure that the same thing is entered right across the table, so you have a line of colours, archangels or Gods, and not a mixture, for it is to these tables that you will need to turn when you start to perform ceremonies (See Table I).

The elements table relates to your Magical Circle, which you will set up in garden or wildwood, under the Sun or the Stars. Natural magic has to be performed out of doors to be one hundred per cent successful, so the

TABLE 1
THE CORRESPONDENCES OF THE ELEMENTS

Please Note: This list is by no means complete, nor is it definitive. There are literally dozens of things which may be attributed to each element and you should seek these out for yourself. Different authors will supply different attributes. Meditate and choose your own.

Elemental Object	EARTH	WATER	FIRE	AIR	SPIRIT
Direction	North	West	South	East	Centre
On altar	Rock	Water	Candle	Incense	
Instrument	Pentacle	Cup	Sword	Wand	
Zodiac	Taurus	Cancer	Leo	Gemini	
	Virgo	Pisces	Sagittarius	Libra	
	Capricorn	Scorpio	Aries	Aquarius	
Season	Winter	Autumn	Summer	Spring	
Time of Day	Midnight	Sunset	Noon	Dawn	
Moon Phase					
Animal					
Bird					
Plants					
God/Goddess from various pantheons:					
Egyptian					
Greek					
Roman					
Celtic					
Norse					
Divination					
Method					
Colour					
Elemental King					
Sense					
Angel					
Power					

Continue adding all the different things you learn about the patterns of a Magical Circle being willing to 'guess' rather than not even attempt to complete the lists. Always enter one item for each element in each line across, without mixing the symbolism. Leave gaps until you are able to fill them up through research or meditation. The gods will actually teach you if you are silent and ready to listen to them sooner you get that idea into your head, and begin to try it out, the better.

INSIDE AND OUTSIDE

If you are working with Nature, you go to her. She is not to be called into some house – for she is far too big, too powerful and too sacred to be limited to your room! What you can do indoors are the rites and exercises which train you: the quiet meditations, the inner journeys, the small magic for your own development – but do not expect mighty forces to turn up at your beck and call, you will have to find the courage to seek them out where they are.

Mental courage is an often overlooked necessity of the modern wild witch, but it is vital. It does feel strange setting up a circle in a garden marked perhaps with small twigs or leaves upon the lawn because you imagine your neighbours will be nosey. They won't! Think about it, how often do you worry about what they are doing on their patch? Do you watch them in case they have suddenly taken up some weird hobby or activity? Do you peep through the curtains at night in case the fire they lit to burn garden rubbish is really a sacrificial pyre? Of course you don't, and nor will they unless you make a great play of your activities. Magic should be secret, so keep it that way, and you will never be disturbed.

The same applies to the wild places, the woods, the fields of remote farmlands, the moors or the shore of the sea at night. Unless you advertise your presence by destroying trees or lighting fires and frightening livestock, no one will notice. I know, I have carried out ceremonies in all kinds of places and no one has ever complained or written to the papers about it. If you ask Nature herself to suggest a good place where you can meet her – and sit still long enough to hear the answer – she will provide a suitable location that you would never have thought of. It will be safe and secret, so long as you wish it.

What so often happens, however, is that through folly, boasting or hinting about your activities, you stir up just the sort of interference and curiosity you really want to avoid. It is a human failing that you should want approval; to be known to be doing something strange and gaining some kind of kudos from that being known. All that has to be firmly quelled for your own sake, and for that of any other magicians in your area. Act silently, secretly and with respect to the wild plants, animals or people around you and the Goddess will care for you, protect you and give you wisdom.

It is important to ensure, if you really want to think of yourself as a natural magician, wild witch or folk mage, that you spend at least part of every day out of doors, becoming aware of what is going on all round you. Most people imagine that you can only meditate indoors, in a darkened room scented with incense, inside a Magical Circle. The opposite is actually true. The greatest Magical Circle which we can enter is the circumference of the Earth herself.

———

Out of doors all kinds of powers and energies are available to us if we gain the confidence to sense and use them. Learn to walk along, under the greatest power of Fire in our world – the Sun – absorbing his energy, feeling his heat and healing powers. Watch your shadow, the play of light and shade making patterns among the leaves of the trees, sparkling on water, reflected from windows and commune with these sources of inspiration. Seek affirmations by asking questions of yourself and seeing flashes of light or patterns of shadow giving you direction. Revel in the heat and light, breathe the energising powers deeply. Breathe out dullness, tiredness and loneliness and inhale heath, vitality and friendship.

CANDLE MAGIC
In the winter you will have time to explore indoor fires, candle magic and the effects of different gums, resins and herbs, burned as incenses. For candle magic, you will need to gather a supply of different coloured candles, including plain white ones, and a variety of different candle-holders and fireproof mats to stand them on. A circle of plate glass over a coloured cloth will reflect its colour around the candle, if you are using this very simple but ancient form of magic.

Within each living flame there is a simple spirit. You can learn to charge a candle by annointing it with almond oil, scented perhaps with vaporizing oils to suit the purpose of your spell. This is done by stroking a tiny amount of oil up the candle, which should be new and chosen for the particular purpose in hand. Make sure you do not get any on the wick. Concentrate for a few moments on attracting a flame spirit who will help you. Take a match and light the candle once it is firmly in the holder. Relax, close your eyes for a moment, allowing your meditative state to take over, and then open them and talk to the candle as if it was a real person. State the purpose of your spell, asking for one thing only. Discuss why you need that kind of help and how you think the matter could best be settled. Allow time for movements of the flame – which should be out of any draughts and not near enough to be affected by your breathing – to answer. Flames can be extremely expressive if you are willing to give them credence. Nods and shimmies, contractions and leanings of the flame can converse with you in a kind of primitive body language if you allow it time to shape itself.

Not only should you observe the actions of the flame but also the patterns it makes, the patches of shadow, the bright aura around it, for each can convey some kind of idea to you. Be willing to accept that very mundane suggestions will be given to you. Magic does not work by angelic forces turning up with gifts on a platter! You will have to gain a rise in wages by working for it; you will have to make new friends by going to places where your sort of people gather, and being friendly.

———

Possessions cost just as much when gained by magical means as they do if you buy them in the marketplace, only you may find exactly what you are seeking with the help of occult methods.

Often when you have sat in conversation with your flame friend for about fifteen minutes you will have some kind of guidance come into your mind and even if it does sound rather ordinary, the chances are it will work. Then you should pinch out the wick, or snuff it with an old-fashioned cone-shaped snuffer, as blowing out candles used in magic is applying breath – the symbol of life – to quench something. With practise, you will soon find that you can pinch out the flame quickly and safely with your fingers.

Fire is dangerous, that is obvious, but many people do not bother to take any kind of precautions, either in or out of doors. If you are taking up magic you must become responsible for your actions, and that means knowing what to do if something catches fire. Learn the correct action in case of fires: like chimneys catching light, oil fires in the kitchen, electrical plug fires and the results of carelessly dropping a match onto the sofa. Make sure you never leave lighted material out of doors, for a small spark could blow onto dry grass or leaves and cause a great deal of damage. A forest fire often results from only a second's carelessness. These days when there are many fallen and drying trees in the woods, such precautions are even more important.

———

Your studies should also include firefighting with extinguishers, water and brooms, and ensuring the safety of any people. Such knowledge could go a long way towards saving the lives of others, and that is a very magical act indeed. You should become aware, as you gain more experience, that you can smell burning, feel heat, or even psychically become alerted to any danger in your neighbourhood. Calling out the fire brigade may not sound very exciting, but your actions could prevent an extremely nasty situation developing into a disaster.

The same kind of practical knowledge should extend to awareness of the dangers of water, caves and jumping off high cliffs. You never know when your awoken sensitivity could benefit others, wherever you are, be it inside a Magical Circle or driving along a road. Become fully attuned to what is real and correct and soon you will be very alert to anything which is wrong, for example, an approaching danger or an accident that is about to happen. That is the practical use of magical knowledge.

Other aspects of fire magic involve knowing a set of correspondences for the seven planets of astrology which equate with the days of the week. Although we are now aware of the outer planets, for the simple arts of old-fashioned natural magic, seven is enough. Make out tables for the days, and complete the various sections (see Table 2). You may be able to look up some of these in other books, but they work just as well if you select relevant things out of your head, and then check later.

TABLE 2: THE CORRESPONDENCES FOR THE PLANETS

Planet	MOON	MARS	MERCURY	JUPITER	VENUS	SATURN	SUN	EARTH
Day	Monday	Tuesday	Wednesday	Thursday	Friday	Saturday	Sunday	Any
Metal	Silver	Iron	Quicksilver	Tin	Copper	Lead	Gold	Any
Colour	White	Red	Light blue	Royal Blue	Green	Black	Yellow	All
Gemstones	Moonstone	Garnet	Opal	Amethyst	Emerald	Jet	Diamond	Agate/All
	Pearl	Bloodstone	Beryl	Lapis Lazuli	Peridot	Onyx	Amber	Semi-precious
Incense	Jasmine	Tabacco	Styrax	Cedar	Rose	Myrrh	Frankincense	Dittany of Crete
God/Goddess from various pantheons:								
Egyptian								
Greek								
Roman								
Number	9	5	7	3	6	8	1	4
Shape	Crescent	Pentagon	Septagon	Triangle	Hexagon	Octogon	Circle	Square
Herb								
Animal								
Bird								
Magical Image								
Symbol								
Angel								
Virtue								
Power								

There are many different attributions published by various authors since the Middle Ages, and each is right for its own time and set of correspondences. You will have to research and complete this table and add to it things which are important to you. For Example, each planet is the ruler of one of the Signs of the Zodiac. Many herbs, incenses, colours and numbers may be attributed correctly to each planet depending on which system is being used, for example the Qabalah. Some systems like that of the Celts, are not so well documented that Gods/Goddesses and symbols are directly associated with each of the planets. Hard work is required to complete and expand this useful Table

You are certain to find a variety of different colours, jewels or plants attributed to each planet, according to which source you read. This is because it is an ancient system which has been developed by a variety of magicians from different schools and traditions.

Choose one system to begin with and change only when and if there is a good reason. If you are sharing your work with others who already have a system, it is as well to accept that to begin with. You need to list: day, planet, colour, number (these vary quite a lot), incense, plants, animals, birds – all to use when drawing up planetary talismans, symbols, tarot cards perhaps, and as many other relevant ideas as you can. This listing should also include the concepts which each planet rules. For example, Venus (Friday) is generally associated with love although really she rules partnerships, of which love is only a part. She will help with any kind of shared venture and it is this aspect of love with which she may be called upon to assist. So do not imagine you can perform 'a love spell' which will only affect the object of your affections! You will always be the primary target of anything you do, and any changes will occur to you most of all. Be prepared!

SYMBOLS, TALISMANS AND SPELLS

It is important to understand the symbols associated with the planets as these form the basis for any actual talismans you might make. A talisman is a 'magical magnet', carefully and individually prepared for a sole purpose. It is not a mass produced item bought from a supplier, no matter what the advertisements may promise! If you need a talisman, you should make it yourself.

In the old days these were very much 'made up as you went along'. They were not usually written on paper, as are many of the modern ones, but inscribed on pieces of wood, slate or tree bark. Each family would have its own marks, or runes. The original runes, about which there seems to be an ever-increasing number of books these days, were twigs or pieces of tree branches with a special shape. In time, these became recognized as a 'sound' or 'letter' of an alphabet. The Celtic people named their letters after the whole tree, whereas the Northern Europeans and Scandinavians used the special shaped twigs. Even today our alphabet contains similar rune shaped letters: T, Y, I, L, E, F and V. Each of these could be a pattern of natural twigs, if you looked for it.

Later these small marks were scratched onto smooth pieces of wood or stone, each originally with straight lines, but gradually special writing instruments were invented so that the familiar curves of 0, S, C and R came into use.

All magicians would make up their own sets of symbols for the kinds of powers they were working with. They would also recognise such natural symbols as the eye, often found on stones or pieces of wood, the phallus, the womb, as well as fossils of spiral snail shells, elf bolts, fairy loaves and holy stones. Each of these turns up in museums of folk life all over the world, along with solar and lunar signs, spirals, swastikas, concentric circles, zigzags and fish scale designs.

Some symbols have a universal meaning, and imply, at a very basic level, some power or protective agency which is called upon. Animal heads are also common as symbols of protection or magic. Mason's marks on old buildings show their own ceremonial tradition survives, and again include special symbols to indicate the name or family of the workman. Here is found the five-pointed star, the pentagram much loved by modern witches.

This, together with the six-pointed star, the hexagram, turns up frequently in magical books. The pentagram is supposed to represent humanity when it has one point at the top, and the animal kingdom symbolized by a horned goat, when the two points are at the top. It is a natural symbol found in any flower of the rose family, within certain fruits – particularly the apple – and has always been looked upon as a protective device and a bringer of luck and immortality. The six-pointed star is the natural shape of all snowflakes, many other flowers and seed pods. Here the design is made up of a descending and an ascending triangle. These have many meanings, but can basically be envisaged as the upward thrusting power of growth, intermixing with the downward pointing energy of the sky or cosmos. Ceremonial magicians,

Pentagram   Hexagram

especially Qabalists, who delineate this symbol on the Tree of Life, use it as a central part of their talisman making. It has also become the device used on the flag of Israel, and in the Jewish synagogues and is an equivalent of the Christian crucifix.

You can spend many fruitful sessions of meditation on both these basic symbols and learn a great deal. This is vital before you start to wear any such device, for to wear a sacred sign you do not fully understand is foolish, to say the least. Every old magical symbol means something very powerful. It is a key, and you will be influenced if you adopt it whether you understand its meaning or not. Do you really want to take on that responsibility without knowing what you are doing?

There are books of formal talismans which must be written on virgin parchment with specially made inks, and coloured with paints, using the sigils of strange demons or Spirits of the Planets: but these are not for the novice, or the person who does not really know what it is all about. It is far safer to 'invent' symbols and work out the wording and concepts using your own modern language, rather than try out something which looks more authentic but whose powers you do not understand, and cannot control. The Gods are wise, they will listen to any sincere prayer and answer any reasonable request, no matter how simply it may be made.

Once made, any sort of talisman needs time to work. You can certainly follow the Moon's phases, making a talisman for increase at the Full Moon and decrease – say of an illness – during the waning Moon. A charm is a natural object, stone, fossil, holy stone or wooden object which is protective. An amulet drives away evil or harmful influences. A charm can also be a spell, that is, a chant or prayer repeated seven times and then forgotten.

Do not use banishing rituals all the time unless you want to drive away love, friendship, health, good luck and so on. You only ever need to banish and clear a space if you obtain a new magical instrument, which might well need cleansing, or to consecrate a talisman during a ceremony. Afterwards always unwind the circle and let life continue unchecked. Many people do perform banishing rites each evening and wonder why they then cannot remember their dreams! Always try to understand thoroughly, and in your own terms, whatever it is that you are doing. Do not take something from another source just because it looks good. The time spent becoming certain that you are doing the right thing will never be wasted.

One very old kind of magical spell is that which uses a magic board. This is a slice of new wood, about a handspan across, onto which you must accurately inscribe a circle containing an exact equilateral triangle which touches the circle at three points. This must be carved with a stone and the wood should not be touched with your hands, but kept wrapped in a clean white cloth. The board should be left out under the light of the Full Moon for a whole night, and out in the sunlight for a whole day, from dawn to dusk. When you wish to make a request for something you must spend three days deciding what it is, and then make your plea very simple and direct. 'Give me a hundred pounds', however, will not work! You have to ask for something you need.

When you have condensed your request into as few words as possible, write them with a new pen on a sheet of clean paper, and touching that with a cloth, fold it in four. Ideally, you need an old-fashioned hat pin or a large thorn which you can use to pin the folded paper to the centre of the triangle, without touching the paper or the pin. You should hold this upright with a twig and tap it into the board with another piece of wood. This may seem complicated, but it is a manner of traditional magic that works, so long as you do exactly as you are told.

———

When the pin is holding the request firmly in the board, ask three times that your request be granted, turn round three times clockwise, and carefully wrap the whole thing in the cloth and place it under your bed at the head end, or on top of a cupboard. Then forget about it. Allow a month to pass and if you have done it right, your wish will be granted, or if it has not been, you will know exactly why not.

All talismans need time to work, for they are changing the nature of time, and like seeds sown in the garden, each has to grow in its own time whether it be a carrot or an oak tree. Do not keep looking at any spell you have created, for that will destroy any hope you may have of its success. If you dig up growing seeds they die, if you keep on interfering with spells, they will not work – that is a law of magic. Forget about the whole matter, concentrate on doing things in the 'real' world, for you have sown a seed on the inner, and there it will grow until it is ready to blossom in your own realm. Be patient. In about 28 days nearly all spells will have shown results of some kind. Then you must destroy the talisman or spell, or remove the written request from the magic board and burn it, saying, 'thank you' three times and turning anticlock wise. If you do not say thank you, even in the case where you did not get quite what you expected (which is real magic!), you will not get any further help. Would you continue to help someone who is ungrateful? The spell board may be kept for a future occasion, but do not be greedy or keep on asking for the same thing, if you do not get it the first time.

Talismans may be made for any purpose, using the correspondences which you have collected and added to the lists in Table 2. Make only one at a time, as if you make several, that will lead to their all failing. Take your time before you spring into action. Draw the talisman on clean paper – it is best if you keep a special drawing pad and a set of coloured pens just for this purpose. You will also need a good pencil, a rubber, a compass and ruler to ensure that circles, squares and other shapes are drawn exactly, for this does matter. If you do not know the proper angelic names of the powers you want help from, use modern English which they all understand very well!

Wrap each one in a clean cloth of the correct colour – silk is by far the best, and a supply of cheap squares may often be obtained in a market. Place the completed talisman on your altar if you have one, or hidden in a tree, or buried under the ground in your garden, and allow it to do its work. Certainly you can invent a ritual to cleanse it of past associations – so long as you take this very seriously – to focus it specifically on your request and to ask the blessing of the Gods, Goddesses or angels before it is set aside, or 'planted' to do its work. Play at any kind of magic and you will be asking for trouble: do it sincerely, and even if you are a novice, you will be surprised as to what you can achieve.

———

Once a talisman has done its work it should be burned or buried, or if it is on a stone, it can be cast into a running stream so that it returns to its original elements. Do not expect other people to make talismans for you, for their needs, will and attitudes, will be different from yours, and the spell will generally work for them first. Do not be taken in by promises of great things from people who advertise in popular magazines either. If they were really good at magic they would not need to advertise products for sale as they would have sufficient resources of their own. The same applies to anything you might think you can buy: wisdom, power, friendship, love and magical abilities have to be earned by good old-fashioned hard work.

There are no short cuts, no 'special offers', no universal good luck charms – each one is distinctly individual. If someone offers to help you, you may need to exchange something: time, energy or bartered goods. You might need to pay for books, training or guidance – but only what you can afford. The Gods will always supply your needs if you offer yourself to their service, but you will still have to work very hard to earn their support!

CHAPTER FIVE

Scents and Sensitivity

If under the night-stars of the desert thou presently burnest mine
Incense before me, invoking me with a pure heart, and the Serpent
flame therein, thou shall come a little to lie in my bosom . . .
MAGIC, IN THEORY AND PRACTICE – Aleister Crowley

Magic is about change, and the awareness and control of that change. The more aware you become, first of what is the usual state of things and then of any changes, the more control you will gain of those changes. It is a matter of perception. If you begin to sense that a tide of inner energy is running in a particular direction, then you can launch the canoe of your desires upon the flood and gain benefit from it. If you suspect the tide is running out, then you can cast up on its fleeting waters those things of which you wish to be rid.

You need to have controlled perception, and to have time in every day's programme to receive any such hints of change. It is a matter both of being still and of attuning all your five ordinary, and hundreds of extraordinary, senses and of being in a permanent state of readiness to take advantage of any flow which will help with those things which matter to you.

In earlier times, people lived much closer to Nature. They determined their tasks by the light of the Sun or Moon, and they kept the natural rhythm of the seasons, growing and resting by turn. We have lost this 'unalarming' clock, working by electric light and eating the fruits and vegetables we choose rather than those the changing seasons provide.

We have become insensitive to the feelings of our own souls, our own hearts and our own minds, taking our programming from the world around us and its artificial mode. This loss of sensitivity has shut us off from the feelings and desires of others, making many people lonely and despairing. Modern housing has cut people off from neighbours, from the village atmosphere of common friendship or even open rivalry. The pace of life has speeded up to such a degree, that we never seem to have enough time to do those things that we want to do; yet time has to be wasted standing in queues, in traffic jams and at supermarket checkouts! What a life! We have lost control, which leads to a loss of will, and there is no magic left.

To begin on the path of realigning ourselves with Nature is not easy, for it is not a road followed by the majority. It can be lonely and feel strange, yet even the first few steps towards a more aware lifestyle can have valuable benefits. Once you take your courage in both hands and state that you want to rediscover the magic which is part of your native inheritance, you will be gently guided in the right direction.

You do have to listen though, setting aside a quiet moment every day, as regularly as sunrise, and be willing to hearken with your soul. Meditation does not need to be a static and silent activity. It is while walking the dog, weeding the garden, making the dinner, or performing any of those mundane jobs, that your mind can wander and you can make use of the time. Do not try such things while operating machinery or driving a car, however, for your own safety and that of those around you!

It is traditional to assist meditational or inwardly focused states of mind by the use of herbal scents. Today we have a vast choice of ways of perfuming our atmosphere, but some are better for ecological reasons than others. The old fashioned method of using natural potpourri is one way, as well as having a few scented flowers in the house, to brighten a dull room and bring inspiration. You will need to experiment as to which kinds of scents you like, and the effects these have on you.

THE LANGUAGE OF FLOWERS
Natural flowers – fresh or dried – may well be the most pleasing method, but if you are buying flowers do

learn how to keep them looking their best for as long as possible. For example, roses need their hard stems crushed, and the addition of a small section of soluble aspirin to their water will make them last. Sweet-scented carnations will bloom for twice as long if you trim their stems a little and stand them in fizzy lemonade instead of tap water. Any good book on flower arranging from the library will give you many other similar tips.

Try to grow your own sweet-scented flowers if you can, as naturally as possible. The few extra pennies spent on good quality seed or plants will be repaid many times over by the brighter, more fragrant flowers. Try not to force plants to flower out of season, for they lose their scent and do not really last very long. Learn when the best months are for each variety and pick some of the finest flowers for use in dried potpourri, or even as incense.

Many flowers can be eaten and add extra colour to salads, for example, rose petals, marigolds or nasturtiums. Some can be candied in egg white and fine sugar to add an extra special touch to a celebration cake or table centre. This might not sound like magic, but these old skills – working with plants for scent, flavour and decoration of food – go back many hundreds of years. Many of the old pagan temples were always decorated with leafy garlands, berries and fruits, and people who came to petition the Gods and Goddesses would bring offerings of flowers, food and spicy cakes – so this is clearly another forgotten aspect of our magical heritage. Garlands of flowers and leaves were always worn, in the days before crepe paper and plastic decorations. Look at the old art of Well Dressing, carried out in the North and West of England. Huge beds of soft clay are prepared, and the picture to frame the well head carefully drawn. The picture is 'painted' by having coloured flower petals, leaves, moss and ferns, berries and lichens pressed into the appropriate place. In this way, an exquisite illustration is depicted which will last for only a brief spell, but which is an ancient and traditional way to give thanks for the life-giving spring of water. You can try this out, on a much smaller scale, and make an offering picture, or simple 'flower talisman', by making a bed of damp pottery clay in a shallow tray or cake tin.

The language of flowers was particularly popular in Victorian times, when every bunch of flowers or posy was carefully designed by the giver, and then examined by the recipient to see what its message might be. Roses were for true love, yet the different colours indicated eternal bliss or a brief flirtation. Rosemary was for remembrance (even Shakespeare mentioned that in Hamlet), and all kinds of blossoms, leaves, ferns and buds indicated a wide variety of affection, from friendship to undying passion.

You can rediscover this forgotten art and send silent messages to those who matter in your life. Just as the Celts' Druid priests could write messages with tree leaves and twigs and the Runic scholars of the North could imprint their stick signs on strips of bark, so can you spell out your hopes and wishes in front of all the world, and they will be none the wiser, unless they recall this gentle old form of communication. You can also leave prayers to Mother Nature in the form of gardens by using whole growing plants rather than cut flowers. You can make circles of protection or healing, or leave messages of love if you do your homework correctly.

PLANTS AND HERBS

Plants are also useful, for example, in food. There are dozens of pot herbs, each able to add its own subtle flavour to a dish. Many are pleasing plants to have about the place, even if you can only run to a window-box. Choose those you most enjoy to begin with, but do sample others when the chance offers. Frequently summer fetes or flower shows have a section on edible plants, and you can often buy different varieties quite cheaply. The local agricultural show is an excellent excuse to take the family out for the day, and to stock up on some rarities, for most of these can be examined, tasted and discussed with knowledgeable plantsmen, whereas a mere packet of seeds might not tell you much. Often, you only really need a couple of plants of each herb, so a packet of seeds might be too much, although they make useful and most acceptable presents and can frequently be exchanged for some other magical item or guidance.

———

Sometimes this can provide a valuable introduction to other people who, as well as having a love and a wide interest in plants and herbs, are seeking a more magical way. There are often courses on the uses of herbs in cooking, bathing and simple medicines, run as evening classes. The municipal gardens nearly always have a section on culinary herbs and there is sometimes a special scented garden for appreciation by blind or disabled people. Get to know the gardener in any such place and you may find a useful ally, who will give advice on cultivation, picking and preserving flowers. and may be willing to sell or exchange varieties and special, rare plants.

Plants, or parts of them, have always been used in natural magic. From its earliest history, humanity has used their fruit, stems, leaves and roots for food, as healing medicines, to keep away harmful insects and cure bites and wounds, and occasionally, as a short cut to an easy death. It is probably this knowledge of plant poisons which caused the church to fear the old herbalists or 'witches' as they named them. Every community would have had an expert in plant medicines able to concoct all sorts of cures for alleviating pain and fever, and for dealing with any infections or septic wounds which afflicted their people. There was no alternative then – no doctor, physician, vet or pharmacist to provide the kinds of modern drugs, linctuses and medical care which we all take for granted. This old Cunning Man or Wise

Woman would have had a valuable place in the village and would have been consulted, not only on matters of the body, but of the heart also. He or she would have preserved a long oral tradition of knowledge about all manner of natural substances and their curative or sleep-inducing qualities. The Wise Ones would know how much of each plant to use, and if someone was seriously ill or badly injured without a hope of recovery, they could produce a potion to bring on the sleep from which there would be no awakening.

Many of the Wise Women were midwives too, so they held the threads of both life and death within their inherited wisdom. Often in those older days, women would die in childbirth, or their babies would die very young, for reasons which have faded into history by now. It was this power which brought some of them into conflict with the church. At one time it would have been the priest who would offer healing – of a spiritual sort for the seemingly demon-driven sicknesses – but it was usually the old Wise Woman who actually tried to cure the sick person or animal. When threatened with forces beyond their control, the followers of the Old Ways could only resort to poisons, to ill-wishing and curses to defend themselves.

MOVING MEDITATION

We 'book-bound and media-swamped' people forget that in pre-TV, pre-radio and pre-literate days, the common people used their minds to inform and guide them, allowing thoughts, plans and the solutions to ordinary problems, to flow quietly into their minds as they performed their every day tasks. This was not separate 'meditation' as we have it today – a special art learned by practice and performed in special circumstances – but a way of preventing boredom and dullness from taking over their lives.

It takes a fair amount of practice to discover that this form of moving meditation can become combined with many ordinary jobs, if you put your mind to it, to fill in those idle moments in between other activities. Anyone who says he does not have time to meditate is overlooking all those unfilled and useless periods during the day, which add up to several hours if acknowledged and then regained in useful contemplation.

Whether you call it meditation, or just prefer to ponder, imagine, day-dream or contemplate, does not really matter so long you employ those idle moments usefully. For example, you may implant a concept about which you require further information or understanding and then allow it to ferment, just at the level of awareness, so that new ideas spring forth the minute you put your attention fully on the matter. This really does work. It is the source of much useful and creative thinking that leads to realisations, to inspiration and to problem-solving. It often opens up whole areas of unknown inner talent and allows such techniques as lateral thinking to emerge. This, in turn, can supply answers to the most recalcitrant problems, if you allow an open mind and an awoken consciousness to get to grips with them. To begin with, it will help to make the conditions as conducive to clear results as possible. This is done by choosing a place which is quiet; outdoors is good, if the weather is reasonable and often far less of a nuisance to the rest of the family than indoors. A stroll by a river, along country lanes, or even, if the shops are closed on Sundays, through the still, quiet and empty city streets, can lead you to a place of peace and pleasant contemplation. A scented garden, a deserted beach, a lonely copse set amid green fields – you would be surprised at the number of relaxing and spiritually uplifting spots you can find if you open your mind to your need for such, and then follow your intuition.

Indoors, it might well help to dim the lights to a single candle flame, put on some relaxing music and burn sweet scented incenses which can uplift or set free that inner wild spirit. The gifts of Mother Nature, however, are to be found anywhere that is slightly off the beaten track, and will supply the quiet background noises of birdsong, thrumming wind through tree branches, the ripple of water and energising draughts of fresh air. Allow these harbingers of intelligence to carry you away from your weary world, to a place of wisdom and appreciation of those inner resources and genuine, unforced feelings of freedom, religious awareness and worship. The more you allow yourself to be still in the presence of Nature, the wider open your subtle senses will become, unhampered by the rush and bustle of the everyday world. Allow yourself to drift, knowing you will be protected by the forces of Nature, if you give her a chance to be your friend.

Ideas should be allowed to well up out of the natural silence, to grow gently and to get caught in the web of your consciousness, woven and expanded through repetition when conditions are at their best. It is not a skill which can be mastered with gritted teeth and muscle-locked determination. You can only open those strong inner doors with a light touch, a relaxed body and a quiet mind. If you try to force them, they will shut so firmly that you will not shift them at all; do not play at causing them to crack open. If you ease the doors open gently and within your control, suddenly you will find that new concepts, understanding and those subtle links, which join familiar areas of knowledge into the seeds of wisdom, will form imperceptibly. You cannot make it happen. It will grow in its own time, if you are patient, relaxed and gentle enough.

The more time you spend in the countryside, or any place where green things prosper and where Nature's other faces can be clearly seen, uncluttered by man-made objects, the more you will learn from those inner aspects of yourself which are your inherited nature. The Moon and the Sun can open doors to psychic powers, to healing of self and the whole world, if you allow each to teach you, quietly absorbing the lessons, written on the face of the Earth, scattered among the night's stars or inscribed on every ripple of the oceans. All these aspects of Nature were the lesson books of our ancestors and they can show us, in far more ways than the flat, sterile pages of books with their printed hieroglyphs, the keys to our place in the Universe. Feel, sense, experience and grow in the light of Nature's own wisdom. Unless you walk in her ways, she cannot teach you, for her powers have to be requested and won by effort and dedication.

You may certainly study the learned books of herbs, their shapes and habitats, their 'virtues' and uses – if you were never taught these things by your grandparents – but a book cannot teach you to look and actually see the green-gold aura that surrounds a healthy plant with the fine rays of energy clearly indicating its healing power. Only by going out in the early morning, crawling on your knees along the dew drenched lawn, eye to eye with the plants, will their true value be unveiled to you.

Learn to accept information, which has manifested secretly from some inner source of knowledge, rather than from the obvious sources of the written page or the TV documentary. Inside us we all have vast data stores, far greater than computers, and all of that information is retrievable if we allow ourselves to attune to it. Plants, animals, the wind, the weather, the stars and the tides can all teach us many things, if we are willing to give them credence as legitimate sources of instruction. It is basically a matter of learning a form of body-language, both to observe how the physical forms of various things relate to their environment, and to listen to our own bodies for what they can tell us more directly.

SHARPENING THE SENSES

You will find, if you open your senses, that the sights, sounds and scents around you convey a great deal – awakening memories, recalling past events and making future connections. Sight can quickly be attuned to see far more than the ordinary person notices, just by consciously looking. Hearing can be sharpened by listening to silence – you will start to hear all kinds of sounds which were just part of the background, once you take off your headphones, turn off the radio and walk quietly in the green places of your world. Meditation is not induced or enhanced by shutting off all the sounds around you, but by being aware of these totally and being able to ignore them. You cannot stop the world or its roar, you can only deliberately teach yourself to overlook it. That is a matter of conscious decision, not of ignoring things, in the hope that their troublesome nature will fade away and stop disturbing you.

The sense of smell, usually totally ignored by human beings (except wine buffs, tea tasters and perfumers!) is a very vivid sense, and is often capable of unlocking deep aspects of memory. The smell of chalk, school dinners and the churned turf of the sports field, can release powerful ancient echoes of childhood and school-days. The scent of certain flowers can revive a long-forgotten love affair, or the garden of a much-loved home. The merest whiff of certain aromas can powerfully trigger memories of past events, places, people and objects because the nose and the sensory scenting areas of the brain are very close together. Think about it. How often have you walked along a street and caught the scent of something which has recalled to you some memory so deeply buried, yet frighteningly real? It brings it all back, sharply into focus and you relive that moment of excitement, fear or joy.

Scents have been recognised as powerful agents for changing consciousness, for altering moods, and as suitable offerings appreciated by all Gods and Goddesses throughout time. Altars where sweet incense could be burned have been found in Stone Age temples in Malta, for example, some with traces of the resins still discernible. In many parts of the world the offering of various things by fire to the Spirits above has formed an important aspect of worship and thanksgiving. Even today in many churches, shrines and temples, Christians and pagans alike make offerings of incense, joss sticks, scented flowers and burnt gums as a common part of their ceremonies. This is not done merely to create a pleasing aroma for the faithful, but as an offering to the deities, carrying their prayers aloft on the scented smoke.

127

INCENSE

Today, anyone following the paths of magic will have to discover for himself which scents he prefers. There are many shops selling specialist mixes of scented materials to be burned on charcoal blocks, or joss sticks and vaporising oils which are heated in special lamps or over radiators in the home. Scented flowers and dried potpourri can also be used to improve the atmosphere or to focus the attention of those who are working some magical spell on the matter in hand. Incenses can easily be blended to suit your own choice of perfume, to attract a particular deity or power, or to attune your inner perception to the mode which is best for divination, healing or meditation. Only by patient experimentation can you find out what suits you – and the tastes of your companions, if you are working with others. Some people like heavy, thick, smoky gums; others prefer light, flowery essences. Some wish to use the woods and resins dedicated to a particular planetary power; others prefer a more gentle background fragrance, working on the scryer's perceptions, relaxing and opening the way to clear sight.

There are a wide variety of incense components which good suppliers will sell separately. If you are new to the study of magic it is best to try these out one at a time until you can judge your individual reaction. For example, some incense smokes can make you cough, others make you sneeze, some catch in your throat and others send you to sleep. Most of the traditional incenses are the gums and resins extruded from desert plants, like frankincense, olibanum, galbanum, copal or benzoin, mastic and myrrh. Some come from Arabia, others from as far away as Sumatra, and these have been imported for religious use from the earliest days of international trade. Many are extracted from the stems or roots of spiny shrubs, so reminiscent of holidays in the sun. Others come from cuts in the trunks of quite large trees, and as well as these exotic resins, gums can be extracted from fruit trees such as cherry or plum, and many of the conifers, especially pine, cedar or fir, which grow in Britain. Other scented woods like sandalwood, apple, lignum vitae, and again pine, are finely ground or chipped and added to incenses. The stems of rosemary, and lavender, bay leaves, poppy seeds, Dittany of Crete – that ancient sacred plant burned in the Olympian Temples to the High Gods – all have their place in the modern magician's cupboard. Each should be separately stored in a dark glass jar with an airtight top for them to retain their scents for many years. A little of each will go a long way, and about half a teaspoon of incense, sprinkled over a block of modern incense charcoal (when it has completed its sparking heating process), will burn for about half to three quarters of an hour.

Most of the traditional woods, gums and resins are dedicated to a specific planetary power. It is worth seeking out a supply of at least six or seven of these, so that you can perfume and dedicate a talisman, follow a pathworking using their symbolism, or attract the energy each rules over to help with your magic. If you make out a list of the planets, completing Table 2 on page 104, you can enter these where they fit. The old herbals, such as Culpeper's, will indicate to which planet each herb is dedicated, so you can extend the possible list a great deal, for many herbs will burn quite sweetly (and some very noxiously indeed), but it is up to you to see which is which!

Here are a few of the most common ones which should be available as kinds of yellowish-brown crystals or powder, wood chips or, in the case of Styrax, a liquid resin:

SUN: Acacia (gum arabic used in cooking), cinnamon, sandarac, bay or rosemary, or most readily available, frankincense.

MOON: Colophony, jasmine or lignum aloes for the Moon Maiden, and catechu for the Hag aspect. Earthy dittany or styrax may also be used for the Moon Mother aspect.

MARS: Dragon's Blood resin or fiery tragacanth or spicy opoponax or even varieties of pepper, curry spices and hot chillies. (Only burn small amounts as these can make your eyes water!)

VENUS: Benzoin, red sandalwood and many of the obvious things like rose petals, lilies and other dried flowers associated with love can be used.

JUPITER: Ammoniacum or mastic work well for this expansive planet, and there are many herbs dedicated to Jupiter, and also cedar wood.

MERCURY: White sandalwood, or again mastic, will aid communication or speed transport.

SATURN: This dark, restrictive planet is honoured by burning evil-smelling asafoetida, myrrh or perhaps lignum vitae, which opens the door beyond death.

There are many more aromatic spices, woods, herbs (and their stems), gums and resins available in specialist shops and mail order suppliers. If you look in your own kitchen you will probably find all sorts of dried herbs and leaves like bay leaves, cinnamon, jasmine flowers, which can be used in tea, and a wide variety of other scented items which can be added to a basic gum or resin base.

From the garden you can collect the woody stems of rosemary, sage, thyme and even mint to sample. Twigs of larch, pine and fruit woods can be carefully dried and then crushed or pounded with a hammer into tiny shreds. The outer leaf cases of balsam poplar smell exquisite as they unfold in spring: sniff your way round these handsome trees, and collect the sticky buds to dry and burn later. They add extra zest to potpourri too, if you like spicy, warm scents rather than flowery ones.

Once you awaken your sense of smell you will discover

all sorts of aromas, pleasant and horrid, all round you. Often the best ones are not expensive perfumes worn by elegant women, but the homely scents of baking bread, new mown grass, leather, weeds or wild flowers and scented trees. The smell of dried lemon or orange rind, which can be burned as it is oily, as well as all kinds of other scents, will awaken the past, even back into previous lives, where people and the environment did not smell as sweet as our sanitized world might to our nostrils.

Discover how many of the familiar scents around you recall childhood, and see if they help you achieve that child like freedom of mind wherein all inner journeys become real, all dragons breathe fire and dreams can be made to come true. See if countryside smells invoke memories of past lives for you; or if the smell of rusty metal, leather, rough tweed cloth, or heather, awakens your sleeping memories. Does the smell of horses and cattle, wet dogs and bracken, hawthorn blossoms and wild roses arouse any old passions, recollections or strange feelings when you encounter them? For these are scents that would have been around in long dead ages, and they well might, if you are willing to trust your eroded senses. Walk in the rain and smell the wet earth, kick up the brown autumn leaves, perfume yourself with Nature's own fragrances from tree and leaf, bud and blossom. Awaken those forgotten memories, and the inner senses of the heart and spirit.

SENSITIVITY

Although in the past many of the old wise folk sometimes used hallucinogenic plants and herbs in their work, these things are dangerous, and no kind of mind-altering drugs should ever be taken by working magicians, witches or occultists today. Magic is the art of controlling consciousness, not allowing any substance or situation to take away total and instant control. Wine is often drunk in rituals, but it is a matter of one cup, containing perhaps half a bottle of table wine, frequently shared among seven to twelve people! Once you begin to discover the alterations in awareness you can bring about by learning to use your natural senses to the full, you will realize that the dulling effects of tobacco, alcohol and any kind of drugs – often even those used for medical conditions – can be reduced and abandoned completely.

Tobacco is especially bad for you as it not only dulls the psychic senses, it also affects your physical body, causing heart, lung and blood problems, and smoking adversely affects all those around you to a significant degree. If you start to care for the Earth, you will also begin to care for her children, be they people, plants or animals. Tobacco is an incense of Mars, so its effects can also be to cause quarrels, disputes and anger. Certainly it is used as a kind of communion among the Native American peoples in their ceremonies and Sweat Lodges – but that is a different matter and a mystery which needs to be seen in its own light. Magic is about control and awareness. If you refuse to be aware of what harm your habits do to your physical body, which after all is the only one you will get in this lifetime, be they smoking, eating the wrong diet or drinking too much alcohol, then you are a fool and should not dabble with magic. Learn to be aware all the time of the benefits of any substances you eat, drink or take in, be they natural or those you or others around you impose on you. Your senses will soon teach you what is best left alone.

This same law applies to mixed incenses, evaporating oils, perfumes or air fresheners. Some of these contain unpleasant substances to which some people are allergic or which may damage the lungs or the ozone layer. Some perfumes are extracted cruelly from living animals, namely musk from musk deer and civet from the rare civet cat. There are synthetic copies of these scents, but if you care about the animals then anything which is related with their suffering should be looked at very carefully. Fur coats are another area of concern, as are the use of seal skin, badger hair for shaving brushes, and so on – think before you buy, for all these creatures are your magical family. Be kind to yourself, treat your body well, awaken your sight, hearing and senses of taste, smell and touch by constant practice, and you will become a magical new person, filled with life and amazing vitality.

PSYCHIC PERCEPTION

As well as all the mental exercises of meditation and visualisation, which you should be practising as often as possible to awaken your inner senses, it is well worth doing a few simple exercises which will assist your other psychic perceptions to become more acute. Psychism is a valuable tool for the wild witch, but like all the other abilities, it must be controlled. Being able to sense atmospheres in old houses is one thing, but to be immediately overwhelmed with faintness, because you have walked past the site of a nasty road accident is another!

You need to make use of a kind of mental key word or symbol by which you can switch on your sensitivity, and also switch it off. Most of the time, for your own mental peace, it should be switched off. When you sit down to meditate and enter that relaxed and aware state, say to yourself; '*I will now be extra perceptive, by the word...* (or the symbol...)'. See how you feel. At the end, always remember to say: '*I will now return my sensitivity to normal, by this word/symbol*'. When you begin to divine with cards or any other system, as part of your personal attunement to that mode of thinking, you can say your word or conjure the symbol to open the doors of awareness. You can increase or decrease your awareness as is necessary, depending on where you are and what you are doing, by making it your Will, and concentrating for a moment on that which switches it on or off.

———

This is particularly useful if you want to discover the history of something by psychometry. Then, if you are given an object by someone else, as you take it you can use your key word and immediately sense the history of the object, or information about its owner, where it came from, and so on. This has to be an immediate response. It is no good allowing time for your ordinary consciousness to interfere. You must speak instantly you touch the object or you will tend, like most people, to allow the rational side of your mind to dictate and make guesses. Psychometry is not guess-work, it is a genuine psychic skill which 90 per cent of people possess to some degree and which all wild witches should go out of their way to train and control. You will find, if your psychic senses are switched on, all kinds of pictures, feelings, images and thoughts flow into your mind the moment you touch the object you are reading. Without trying to organise these neatly, speak them out loud to the person who you are reading for. It may come out as a jumble, but it is far more likely to be accurate than what might come out in order.

You can try out this skill by visiting antique shops or markets and by touching those old items you find there discover, amazingly it might seem, quite a lot about their history, previous owners and the place they come from. If you relate this information to the dealer, he will possibly be able to confirm your impressions. You might well surprise him by what you can say about the old table or picture which takes your interest. It can sometimes be tried in museums, if you are allowed to touch the exhibits. Here, though, you do tend to pick up information about other visitors, rather than the actual object.

You can expand your awareness to natural things too. It is here that the greatest surprises will emerge. Touch a tree, whilst in a sensitive mood, and you will discover a great deal of its power, its personal energies and character. The same applies to old rocks, crystals and even whole mountains, if you find a place where humans have not interfered too much. Learn to be especially aware of atmospheres: in modern houses, in ancient places you might visit, and around people you meet each day. This is a far more gentle way of assessing their feelings than blunt questions. Gradually, you will find that under your own control you have a deep perception of the moods, emotional state and underlying mental condition, which in some cases may be too deeply buried for the other person to be aware of himself. Through the touch of your hand you can not only receive impressions, but you can send back gentle thoughts of sympathy and care, of support or strength. In this way your silent message will sink deeply into the inner awareness of the troubled person and reassure and calm him, in a way that mere words or conventional gestures may not approach.

Sense the feelings of plants, gardens, moonlight, the wind, and even birds and wild creatures. If you learn the arts of Nature, she will allow you a much closer contact with 'wild' animals than you would imagine was possible. You must have, however, the silence and patience to be in their territory in an unthreatening way, and to send out peaceful and kind thoughts. You can practise this skill with domestic animals, too, by sending out thoughts to cats and dogs. You may be fascinated by their reaction, because most animals are naturally psychic and pick up data from that sense just as they do from their senses of smell, sight and touch through their whiskers. Instead of making silly human noises, send out a mental purr, or a quiet woof, or even feelings of warmth and come hither gestures. These work with young children too, if you try. You can even send gentle waves of 'go to sleep' vibes at fractious babies, and soothe them mentally. This works on trains with other people's youngsters as well, and can be a great relief to all within earshot on occasion!

Do extend your senses, in every way you can, but also learn to switch them into neutral, if conditions suggest this is wise. Learn to trust your sixth sense – and the other twenty or so you can discover with practice.

CHAPTER SIX

IMMANENT DEITIES

*Thou that art One, our Lord In the Universe, the Sun, our Lord
in ourselves whose name is Mystery of Mystery, uttermost being
whose radiance, enlightening the worlds, is also the breath that
maketh every God and even Death to tremble before thee –
By the Sign of Light appear thou glorious upon
the throne of the Sun ...*

MAGIC, IN THEORY AND PRACTICE – Aleister Crowley

The first thing to acknowledge when working with God forms is that these are real. They may not be physical as our bodies are, they may not be visible in ordinary circumstances, yet within their own realms – which you might wish to consider as other dimensions – they are totally real, solid and all-powerful.

There are also a great number of Gods and Goddesses, both those from the past classical religions of Ancient Greece, Rome and Egypt, and those misty and mysterious beings worshipped by the pagan Celts, the Northern folk and in many other parts of the Western hemisphere. Even today followers of the Hindu religion, the Buddhists, and many Eastern branches of these great and ancient faiths, share the concepts of many Gods and

Goddesses, as did most of the aboriginal peoples across the globe. It is really only within the Judaeo-Christian religion and among the Muslims that there is only one God, Father of Creation – although there are many prophets, saints and a Messiah, perceived as Jesus the Nazarene, or yet to come, according to doctrine.

What you accept in terms of deity will be entirely your business. If you are satisfied, content and fulfilled by your religious beliefs, traditions, dogma and practices, that is wonderful. If you are not content here are some ideas for you to think about.

The first concept, as far as religion among wild witches and other serious occult students goes, is one of knowledge, not belief. If they write or talk about angels, Gods or Goddesses whom they work with, that is because it is a statement of fact – for they are talking about beings who are as real as their accountant or bank manager. They will have discovered, probably over many years of meditation, reading and study of the hero tales and the pagan religious texts from many parts of the world, and also by direct appreciation, the reality of the deities they worship and request help from.

They are continuing an ageless tradition which acknowledges that if there was a Father of Creation, there had to be a Mother from whom that Creation sprang. From the Cosmic union came forth all living beings, and thus we are kindred people, animals, plants, each evolving from the stuff of Earth and converted by

Gods or time into living things. We are all related to the planet on which we dwell and each of its life forms, for we are all made up from elements of chemicals, minerals and organic compounds, individually processed to make us either a human being, a ring-tailed lemur, an oak tree or a crystal of Kyanite.

How you construe the idea of evolution is another personal concept. It could be true that some accident of the weather on the surface of the primary Earth set in motion evolutionary changes which through the aeons led from the first amoeba (which still exists, as it grows by division and not by sexual reproduction, each new amoeba being a clone of its parent), to all the dinosaurs and extinct creatures of the fossil ages, to the animals and plants we see all round us. It could be that what has happened to change dull blobs of living matter into seemingly intelligent, world-altering people, was sheer chance.

That is one possibility, but it is rejected by most occult students because they see that the steps in evolution needed a helping hand here and there along the path towards modern existence. The change that caused a dinosaur to grow effective wings and take to the air, the change to live birth as well as egg-laying in many creatures needed outside help. Read any book on the evolution of the species and make up your own mind. Use your growing talents of meditation to examine each step, and if you have mastered the art of Time Travel, go back and look at the lifestyle of Tyrannosaurus Rex or Megatherium, the first cave dwellers and mammoth hunters. This is all fertile ground, only touched upon by novelists and film makers.

OF GODS AND HEROES

Every evolving culture needed its Gods and heroes, too. Once people settled down they would discover a spring of water which not only quenched the thirst but seemed to help the healing of poisoned wounds, or sore eyes, dimmed by crouching over smoky fires. Secret places were chosen deep inside the Earth Mother herself where our ancient ancestors reverently laid out their dead, coloured red as in life and surrounded by their prize possessions, ready to return to live on in some afterlife. Look at the elaborate customs of the Ancient Egyptians. whose literate culture has left us clear records of the lives of the Gods and their worshippers. Look at the vast and glorious temples, sacred areas and buildings, all constructed to honour the Gods of the classical times, and in many places there are even older, more magnificent ruins to be found – in Zimbabwe, at Stonehenge, in Chaldea or in the area of the Indus Valley. These are the forgotten sacred places whose writings and buildings have not yet yielded up their secret wisdom, yet whose power, strength and beauty can be appreciated by us today if we look hard enough.

What you will basically need to think about are

---

a number of concepts which will be personal to you. These include: 'Do I need a God at all?'; 'How can I understand a variety of Gods and Goddesses as I have been brought up in a faith which teaches there is only one God?'; 'What are Elementals?'; 'Is there life after death?'; 'What about praying to saints as I have been taught, or invoking angelic forces as books on magic suggest?'; 'How can I encounter these Beings and understand them for myself?'

Dion Fortune is often quoted as having written, '*All Gods are One God, all Goddesses are One Goddess, and there is One Initiator*'. This seems to imply that all Gods and Goddesses are the same, and that all are subject to some great Creator, but in practical terms this is not quite true. All the perceived Gods and Goddesses worked with by those experienced in magic are real, separate and individual. They may in their own realm be aspects of one God and one Goddess, but as far as we humans are concerned, limited by our human vision and understanding, they are different beings; to be approached carefully and with respect.

One of the commonest mistakes which a novice working with pagan deities makes, is to assume that because he knows something about Isis, a bit about Odin and some more about Jupiter, that these can conveniently be combined into one ritual. That is asking for the sort of trouble which turns out as mental confusion, making errors and not getting the kind of response that is hoped for.

Each pantheon is separate. If you are working with the Gods and Goddesses from classical Greece, stick to them, burn their incenses, and at least greet them in Greek (oh yes, all the Gods speak different languages too!). Most of them will understand you if you speak to them clearly in your own tongue, certainly, but you will need to enter their landscape, their home temples and their sacred precincts if you expect them to help you, and there they will speak their own language. How is your knowledge of pre-dynastic Egyptian, early Celtic or Atlantean, come to that? A word or two could come in handy, but there aren't any Astral Travel Phrase Books that I have come across!

If you are following the path of natural magic, the problems are reduced to some extent, for the deities you will mostly need to deal with are the Earth Mother and her consort/son, the Lord of the Wild. In classical terms you will have to discover who these may have been, although many people are familiar with Pan, whose name means 'all' in Greek. He was the half-goat, half-man God of all wild creatures, the 'shepherd of goats upon the wild hill's way'as one poet put it. He is a character who turns up in such diverse contexts as *The Wind in the Willows*, that famous children's book by Kenneth Grahame, as 'the piper at the gates of dawn', and in science fiction and traditional horror stories.

He gave us the term 'panic' and is not one to be taken lightly, even in our civilized settings. Pan is guardian of all wild creatures, he is their champion and master. He is still visible – if you dare to enter the untouched wilderness, going alone at sunrise with a suitable offering of fruit or flowers and sitting silently in the misty, pre-dawn light. Wait until the beating of your heart almost chokes you, and the merest rustle in the undergrowth petrifies you, and when you are overwhelmed by the twin passions of joy and terror, then you might know that Pan is coming. '*Horn and hoof of the Goat foot God ... We speak the spell thy power unlocks, at Solstice, sabbat and equinox ...*' to quote part of a magical invocation by Doreen Valiente.

Nature is wild, her powers are beyond our ken or understanding yet if we really want to master the Old Arts we are going to have to go to the deserted places, the deep woods, the quiet sea shore and the lonely moors to experience those forces for ourselves. Too many people play at being pagans or witches, never for one moment really accepting that the forces they invoke in their tame, indoor circles are anything more than the words of pretty poetry in a book. They will not realise they are sowing the wind, and sooner or later they will reap a whirlwind, for these powers, conceived by us as God forms, are immanent, potent and overpowering. Nature will treat her children with care, but she still wreaks occasional havoc with floods, storms, tempests and droughts. These are not punishments, but ways of reminding us that we are in her thrall, no matter how clever and 'advanced' our technology. We are still as powerless as babes when it comes to wind or weather, tide or season.

———

ELEMENTAL BEINGS

Some magical books write also of Elementals, saying these beings are untrustworthy, dangerous and difficult to deal with. Most books do not mention them at all, except the heavy Qabalistic tomes, which name their Kings as: '*Ghob, the King of Earth; Nixsa, the King of Water; Djinn, the King of Fire; and Paralda, the King of Air.*' That doesn't tell us much at all. Some people who have tried to understand the nature of Elementals have sought them out, usually in the safety of their own homes (where few Elementals are likely to be found), and wondered why their visions are dim and unhelpful. Think about it. The Elemental King of Water rules all waters, seas, oceans and great rivers, as well as streams and springs for whom, as has been stated before, there are guardian Goddesses as well. He is hardly likely to turn up to preside over a small bowl of tap water or a goblet of wine! Especially if you order him about, or expect him to perform party tricks to entertain your coven.

The Lords of the Elements are vast figures whom we can normally only interact with in the vaguest way. They are beings of another dimension, another scale of things. If we take ourselves to their realm as it is on Earth and ask politely that the Lord of Air, for example, visit us for communion, or to instruct us in some remote and windy place, he might be willing to do so. You probably will not see him, except in the vast patterns of clouds soaring overhead, but you may well hear the roar of his voice and if you are polite and listen, he will instruct you. Hearing is attributed to the sense of Air, just as touch is attributed to Earth, taste to Water and sight to Fire.

Elementals may be thought of as lesser spirits, but they are still powerful and playful beings of totally another order of Creation to our own, so they should not be called up from their realms just to prove they exist. You should have a very good reason before calling upon them, and you will need to find a place at the borders of your safe realm and theirs. All the ancient deities can best be encountered 'between the worlds'. In some books on witch rituals it is stated that 'the circle is a place between the worlds'. So it is, but it is not achieved in reality by merely reading the words of some rite out of a book, lighting a few candles and sprinkling salty water about the place.

'BETWEEN THE WORLDS'

Casting the circle is, in fact, a dramatic and potent start to any ritual, wherein the ordinary earthly place is altered, by the controlled will and creative vision of the magician, actually to be perceived as different. There are lots of people who play at ritual, acting it out without giving one iota of feeling or commitment to what they are doing. This is just play acting and that is all. To make it work, to make the consecrated circle become a 'place between the worlds', you have to build that image so strongly that it is indeed what you see: a circle, floating in space, limited by the power of your will. You do not set it up, bless it with the elements and then wander in and out as if it were invisible and unreal, as so often happens with those who are only mildly interested in what they are doing.

You need to be in a state of 'between-the-worldsness' too, so that the reality of the circle, its symbols and its golden fire-rimmed edge are the total of your perception for the time of the working. In this state, you are no more likely to step outside that circle of flame than step over the edge of a cliff! At the end of the ceremony, you will need time and effort to relocate that circle of space back into the hole in your world from which it-has been temporarily borrowed: and make sure it fits! You will need to switch yourself thoroughly back into your everyday self too. Because the space of your magical ring is taken out of the world, it will not be invaded unless you are totally mad and have invited all your acquaintances along to watch from outside, or you are conducting a ritual on a well-frequented foot path! A Magical Circle will remain inviolate if it is laid out properly and with sincerity; no one will enter it or disturb you so long as you are acting sensibly, in or out of doors. It may sound far-fetched that you would seem invisible to anyone passing by, but it is a fact.

APPROACHING THE GODS
You will need to decide, through meditating on the

various Gods and Goddesses, whom you intend to dedicate yourself to. You may choose the simple idea of the Lord and Lady of Creation, naming them as you will – for this is safe and they will answer you as simply and directly as you address them. If you prefer to adopt a more ancient pantheon, you will need to do your homework very thoroughly first. Even the most innocent-seeming deities have powerful aspects, which act far beyond what we mere mortals might imagine they can do.

You will have to know their stories from the traditional myths and legends of your chosen land, to learn who the heroes were, the humans who worked with the Gods in times gone by, and who the deities themselves were. You will need to understand the names we tend to call them, what they mean and what that title actually implies. Most of the God names are closer to what might now be called a 'job description', not a personal name. It is very important to understand exactly what each is responsible for, who among the other deities they are related to, where they fit in to the whole pantheon and in what manner they were worshipped in their own age.

The Old Gods do not go away; it is we who have forgotten how to make a journey to their Olympian realm, to Valhalla, or to the Underworld where many Gods go to be renewed in the arms of the Earth Mother, and many heroes venture to wrest treasures from the dark places under the Earth – where time is ended, and strange monsters have their being. All these can be encountered, if you set out upon the hero's journey, for you will need to be brave and daring to visit the Gods in their high homes, or deep and secret places across the River of Forgetfulness.

Many have visited the Old Ones, to ask favours, to see into the future, to gain jewels or special knowledge. Each of these things may be gained, but it will have a price. Odin, the Norse God of Knowledge, hung for nine days and nights in an ash tree until he understood the patterns of the branches and saw them as the runes we are rediscovering now. Hungry and thirsty, bound by his own will and wounded with his own spear, he was caught in the branches of the World Tree until it revealed its secret of writing to him. That is a traditional way of approaching the Gods – with fasting and prayer, by returning to the wilderness for forty days and nights, or by making offerings and sacrifices.

In this respect, a great deal has changed. Modern people recognise that they have nothing to offer which is not part of the Earth and part of Mother Nature herself, except their own ambitions, dedication, time and effort. Cruelly sacrificing animals, offering blood or anything more alive than some fruit or a flower is not part of magic. It probably never really was. If you ever encounter any magical group that says a sacrifice of anything living is needed, back away fast and tell the authorities. We offer only incense, wine, honey, milk or flowers today, and our magic is as powerful as ever. We offer our own work and energy in order that the Great Work of evolution may proceed. Be very careful if you are expected to provide blood for any kind of ritual. It is not a part of any modern system and can be very dangerous, for blood, like hair or nail clippings, can form a link between you and any forces – for good or ill. Be very careful indeed, if any such thing is asked of you. If you are making a talisman for yourself, to be under your own control and chosen for your own purpose, you can certainly build the link with yourself by enclosing a few strands of hair or a drop of your blood, but do not let anyone else do it on your behalf!

Magic is ethical. That simple fact is very hard to get through, particularly to a media hungry for excitement, nude dancing and strange ritual sacrifices. Those things, on the whole, are fiction. Certainly there are some covens of witches whose worship involves secret, indoor ceremonies, where all participants are naked, or 'skyclad'. That is part of their tradition, but there are many, many more groups who meet in or out of doors, robed in special garments that are kept for the sole purpose of magical work. These may be as simple as a kaftan, or as elaborate as embroidered robes; they might just be a special coat, or a scarf used to switch the individual into his worshipping and magical self. You must choose from the different paths, but if you follow the Old Gods of Nature, you may dress how you like, meditate or perform spells and rituals as you like, so long as you do not harm the countryside, upset animals or make a nuisance of yourself.

Explore the myths and legends which appeal to you. They all contain the Mysteries of religious and initiation rituals. The hero is the seeker who sets out from his ordinary world to gain a treasure, overcome a monster, rescue someone and so on. These are all allegorical versions of the quest by the modern magical student to discover his own powers, develop skills of mind and spirit and overcome aspects of his own being. These stories have endured through many hundreds of years because they still strongly appeal to us, and their ancient message is just as relevant to us today. Each person has to choose how he will interact with his deity, either in the orthodox manner of the Father God, who demands worship and praise, or in the pagan sense of the many aspects of deity, seen as individual Gods and Goddesses.

It is important for you to make up your own mind about deities. Some people have to envisage Gods and Goddesses as kinds of superhuman people with glorified bodies, minds and spiritual attributes. Some perceive them as vast beings, stretching across the sky or sea. Others see them as very homely forms, almost like ordinary people to whom it is natural to turn for help and advice. What manner of form they take to you must be the result of your own studies and meditations. It is equally possible to 'see' them as having no physical form at all, but being vast fields of energy which can act in particular ways. They may be perceived during a ritual, for example, as great pillars of light or fire, whirling clouds of vapour or almost invisible forces which have no recognizable shape at all.

Each will work, but it must be the result of co-operating with the force that is personified by a particular deity, and not a matter of blind faith because someone else insists on dictating what a Goddess looks like. All these beings are shape shifters, what we see is what we have created for them to inhabit. Their forms are derived from our in built ideas as to what certain Gods and Goddesses are described as, in classical sources.

The Celts did not personify their deities at all, and did not carve statues or representations of them, until they came under the influence of the Romans, whose God statues were to be found in every place they conquered. In many places, the Romans took over the local deities, linked them with Gods of their own pantheon, and then made images of them. Again each was portrayed as a kind of superhuman, not the energy or force which the older pagans might have construed it as. The famous carvings of the Celts tend to be abstract patterns often based on spirals and circles, and occasional carved stone heads – often with several faces – which represented certain aspects of their secret tradition, perhaps signifying the concept of several layers of self within one body, or many different lives.

UNDERSTANDING RELIGION

It is important to discover your own understanding of the function of religion. It comes from the root word meaning 'rule'or 'regulation' and so offers a plan by which to organise your life. It also offers, in its own way, a code of morality, ethics and behaviour. Much of the Judaeo-Christian code is governed by rules that state, 'Thou shalt not ...' whereas it has been suggested that most of the new varieties of philosophy or religion offer a 'free-for-all' lifestyle. This is not actually true. Again the popular press has misunderstood the concept of 'True Will' to mean 'do as you like'. However, True Will is an important concept in Western Magic, and the opposite, in fact, is nearer the truth. Crowley's often quoted *'Do what thou wilt shall be the whole of the Law...'* derives from Rabelais, a sixteenth-century French philosopher, and originally St Augustine. The most common mistake is to suppose that the 'thou'referred to is yourself: but that is not the case. It is the Divine Will that first has to be sought and then complied with.

Conventional religions stress the need to keep the sabbath day holy, whereas to the broadly pagan or unorthodox believer, all days are equally holy, and some days also merit special celebration. The same concept is valid about places. To the average Christian, the place you go to talk to God is a church, on a Sunday, where a specially trained priest will conduct prayers, offer communion and direct your religious activities.

The pagan path is rather the opposite, holding that every individual is his or her own priest or priestess, in direct and immediate contact with God, or the Gods and Goddesses of a particular pantheon, wherever and whenever a need is felt to awaken that contact.

Buildings made by man are artificial limits to the power and glory of deity and it is often preferred, especially among those who follow natural magic, always to be out of doors under the Sun or Moon and Stars. Here the things which you see, if you raise your eyes to heaven, are those things made directly by the Creator. It is by the trees, rocks and streams, under the stars, and in the sunshine of the natural environment, that it is possible to approach that Creative Spirit – where the wind can hear your prayers and the smoke of incense safely carry them aloft.

It is also important to recognize that there are many different aspects of religious activity, especially if you are having to re-assess your complete set of ideas on the matter. You can discover a whole range of activities which are legitimate aspects of all religions, and which you may perform for yourself. These include prayers which are essentially requests for a physical objective, or for healing, or for knowledge. There are songs or hymns of thanksgiving when something good has happened or when a prayer has been answered. In the ancient world, many small altars dedicated to the various local pagan Gods have been discovered, which are offering thanks from some grateful supplicant. It is an excellent idea – not maybe to carve an altar stone, but to plant a garden, or even a single plant, as a thank you.

Another aspect of many religious practices is that of communion, where some kind of sacred meal is shared between the congregation and the priest. On your own, you will need to pour libations of wine onto the Earth, and scatter crumbs to honour the Old Gods or the Spirit of Nature.

You will have to sort out the matter of sin and forgiveness. In most magical schools these are interpreted in a rather different way to that of the Christians. Most magicians do not accept the idea of 'original sin', feeling that our faults and failings are things which on Earth, in one life or another, we will have to put right. Darkness is an absence of light, not a separate substance; sin is an absence of good, a mistake, or a deliberate act against the flow of evolution perhaps, but it can often be put right. Forgiveness has to come from inside following a feeling of guilt or distress, as a result of something we have done, but it is up to us, within the laws of karma, to put it right. No external force, priest or God can correct what we have spoiled, it has to be our own efforts which redeem the balance. Under the laws of karma you cannot pass the buck or pretend you were not responsible.

Responsibility is another, unbendable law of magic. If you cause things to go wrong, from ignorance or folly, then it is you who will have to restore them. There are no excuses. You are not judged and condemned by some harsh Father God: but you must see your own mistakes unshaded, in the light of knowledge, and then you must pay the retribution. It is the best argument against harming other people, or trying to bend them to your will, for as they may be hurt, so will you suffer; and as they may be bent so will you be!

The magician uses prayer a great deal, often punctuating every day with a number of observances. It is an excellent practice and good training to allow your life to mesh into the cogwheels of Nature.

Each day at sunrise, noon and sunset, you should spend a moment of silent contemplation, marking time in your daily round to acknowledge the passing hours, the patterns of the seasons, your thoughts and aims, your inner wishes and silent thanks. It takes only the blink of an eye, the momentary bowing of the head to realign yourself regularly to the world in which you live. These sessions can be prolonged into brief periods of meditation, or small rituals to mark the beginning and ending of each day, with its aims and its achievements celebrated in due time. It can be time to ask for help, for strength, for patience or endurance – as the moment requires – and seldom are these requests unheard.

You can attune to the cycles of the Moon and the Sun, and celebrate formally, the solar journey through the Zodiac, or the waxing and waning currents of Lunar power. You can discover a whole list of reasons to mark many days each year with a ritual, or remembrance, or rite of passage if you wish. But it is always important to understand how the subtle relationship you have with your chosen deities can be enhanced and made stronger. It is not a matter of believing anything, or of having faith, but of developing personal experiences which are your own indication that there is someone there to hear your petitions. Only personal and individual dedication can awaken that slender link from the here and now to the eternal. It cannot be truly forged by any priest, nor any other individual on your behalf. You have to go, for example, out under a summer sky and ask to be accepted as a Child of Earth, or a Devotee of Isis, and you have to wait for an answer, and be prepared to live with the consequences for the rest of your life.

The commitments of magic, be they as a result of initiations into a group or school, or arrived at as an individual act, are forever. They are unbreakable. Certainly you may part from the group and choose to walk a different path as a result of your expanding knowledge, that is a frequent occurrence, but you will be held to your promise through the rest of this life. It is an excellent reason to be very sure you know what you are letting yourself in for before committing yourself to some coven or philosophy which may not prove to match up to the high ideals you had to begin with. Caution is never wasted. If you swear some kind of allegiance to any principle you are stuck with it. Ignore the consequences of breaking your word at your own peril. Think very hard before you perform any act of magic so that you do not live to regret your hasty action. Time is always on your side, and a better option will almost always present itself if you are willing to trust the Gods.

OUR SACRED CENTRE

Each of us is born with a Divine Spark inside us, and by becoming aware of that link with the Creator, we can achieve great things. Each of us is a ruler of our perceived universe; each of us can change the future, heal the sick, improve humanity's lot, if we so will and if we have the courage and wisdom to know what is right. Each of us, in a small way, can do amazing things through aligning our will to that of evolution, growing in light, defeating the darkness of inertia, decay, lethargy and despair. We may find that part of our work in these healing arts has to be in the world, working physically among the disadvantaged, the starving, the homeless or the insane. Others will discover that some of these troubles can be tackled at a different level, in the world of the Gods and Goddesses of Healing, Peace and Plenty. The Earth Mother is fruitful, she can restore the Wasteland, if we help where we can, and bring sufficiency where there was hunger, whether for physical or spiritual food.

In the ancient past the people discovered places which were of themselves sacred. They discovered the existence of Spirits, Dryads, Elementals, Gods and Goddesses associated with the particular places or natural things, and gradually found ways of communicating with them to ask for help, for healing, for guidance and for inspiration. Modern religious practice overlooks all those aspects of observance, setting up new buildings in convenient places, not specifically aligned with the energies of the Earth. These new churches are often mean, temporary structures, built as commercial enterprises, ruled over by preachers whose aim is self-aggrandisement, not honest worship and communion with God. Send money to prevent the preacher being carried up to heaven? What a stupid message that is to fall for. If his God is merciful, glorious, and heaven is beyond imagination, should he not wish to get there as soon as possible?

Look at the land around you. Learn to see the shapes of great Goddesses lying among the green hills, see the guardian shapes in cliff and tree trunks, sinuously winding in water courses, ruffied by the winds of air. Every natural place is a sacred centre filled with aspects of the Life Force. Every human being is imbued with a Divine Spark which, given encouragement, can be fanned into a blaze of Holy Glory.

Many people have grown up without the rule of spiritual awareness, and this shows so clearly in mundane situations. They have no concept of right and wrong, no personal responsibility for their actions, no awareness of the other dimensions of being, and they spend their lives in pursuit of pleasure, or at least the dulling of unacknowledged pain with drugs, alcohol and abuse of others. We need a spiritual revolution to awaken the love of life within people, to help them perceive their divine ancestry, their immortality, their powers of good and evolution.

Each of us must rediscover our personal relationship with the sacred within ourselves and within the world. We must open the doors of awareness by the invocation of Self and through communion with Self, with our Holy Guardian Angel, our God-selves. We must give thanks and be willing to strive for the things which matter, sacrificing time and effort for the good of Creation. This Earth can be paradise, its wounds can be healed, its people fed, its lands returned to their fertility and lushness, if we dedicate ourselves on all levels. First, to understanding the problems, and then to seeking real and enduring solutions on the physical, mental, spiritual and most holy levels. Those sacred beings, the Immanent Deities, of all cultures and all pantheons will teach us – if we will listen.

PURPOSE, PATTERN AND PERIMETER
You might find it helpful to develop a personal structure which can be used as the framework for any meditation session, up to a formal ritual with many participants. Each part may be a simple affirmation or statement, or

it may be an elaborate prayer, poem, song or invocation, with several participants saying something. It may be silent, acted out by mime or gesture – as many ancient rites were – so that the ordinary people saw a kind of dance, whereas the trained initiates perceived the actual meaning. (Look at any picture of Egyptian rituals: there you will see the magical gestures clearly depicted.) Every magical or religious act must have a purpose, a pattern and a perimeter, of either time or space, be it 'to meditate on the symbol of a rose', or 'to invoke the healing power of the Goddess of Earth to restore the deserts...' The purpose is for you to decide – make a simple and clear statement silently or aloud at the commencement of the working and at the conclusion, to concentrate the work.

The pattern is the structure of words, movements, blessings, communion, prayers, offerings of incense, consecration of talismans, meditations and anything else necessary, including the raising and closing of a circle and a final act of thanksgiving. The perimeter is the limitation – the physical circle which, once set up and blessed around you, should be treated as if it were made of red-hot barbed wire with a million volts going through it! It can also represent a period of time, like 15 minutes for a meditation or nine days for a Novena of special prayers, lasting right through each day and night. (Magical Novenas are often seven days long rather than nine, one for each planet, but it is the same process. Each day represents a step forward in the process of ritual dedication, healing, or whatever other purpose such a major working might have been set up for.)

Here is an example of a basic structure which can be modified to suit each individual:

1. Begin by making yourself holy or aware of who you are – perhaps by saying a prayer of self-blessing, by making a gesture, or by putting on your magic robe.

2. Cast the circle, blessing each quarter in turn with the appropriate element, and lighting a candle or calling upon the Power, Angel or Guardian.

3. State your purpose clearly and unequivocably.

4. Leave a moment for thought about what you have said.

5. Perform any ceremonial acts, consecrations, invocations of higher powers, divinations, healing rituals, self initiations and so on.

6. Wait for some sort of response. Offer more incense, perhaps.

7. Share a co-union according to your tradition.

8. Meditate for a little longer. Think of anything you had forgotten to make clear to your companions, or the Gods and Powers you are working with.

---

9. Say 'Thank you'. and mean it. (Just because you do not always get instant visible results does not mean you have not had instant assistance!)

10. Have a final think, ensuring you have done everything you intended. You can still await some kind of response by word, symbols, inspiration and so on.

11. Unwind the circle slowly, ensuring that each quarter is thanked and appreciated. Snuff out the candles.

12. Restate the purpose firmly – if you have had an answer, say so, and be grateful and respectful to any beings whose help you have requested.

13. Clear up inside the circle, remove your own magical self, disrobe and scatter the incense ashes and the dregs and crumbs of the communion onto the Earth. Wash up the sacred vessels and put them away, hang up your robes and write up your magical journal, stating time, place and objective. Later you will need to add results or outcome! Finally, have a cup of tea or a drink of fruit juice and a small snack – fruit is best – to ensure you feel 'normal' again.

Any place can become holy, any words sacred, the Deities will help if there is a good reason, and their powers are limitless. Learn to use intuition, to give thanks spontaneously, to attune yourself a few times each day to the eternal forces of Nature, and your life will be renewed – you will be inspired, guided and granted wisdom in ways you cannot imagine, whatever your religious direction may be *'ask and it shall be given unto thee, knock and it shall be opened...'*

It is well worth writing out the stages of the pattern and fitting into each section a list of what you have to do, what you (or a companion) has to say, what objects – like candles, wine, corkscrew, matches and so on – you need at each stage (and which cannot be fetched from outside once the circle has been consecrated – mime, if you have to!). You can tune the ritual as you need – for Thanksgiving, as a Seasonal Celebration or a simple self-healing rite – so long as you think all the time about what you are doing, and why, and act sincerely and respectfully.

Any place can become holy, any words sacred, the Deities will help if there is good reason, and their powers are limitless. Learn to use intuition, to give thanks spontaneously, to attune yourself a few times each day to the eternal forces of Nature, and your life will be renewed – you will be inspired, guided and granted wisdom in ways you cannot imagine, whatever your religious direction may be. 'Ask and it shall be given unto thee, knock and it shall be opened . . .'

CHAPTER SEVEN

SEASONS, CYCLES AND FEASTS

*Let the rituals be rightly performed with joy and beauty! There are
rituals of the elements and feasts of the times ... A feast for the
Supreme Ritual, and a feast for the Equinox of the Gods.
A feast for fire and a feast for water; a feast for life and a greater
feast for death! A feast everyday in your hearts in the joy
of my rapture!*

MAGIC, IN THEORY AND PRACTICE – Aleister Crowley

We are deprived, not only of the lost heritage of magic from our lives, but also the joy and celebrations of life. Our work schedule may be punctuated with bank holidays, religious feasts or national holidays which break the dull, daily grind, but we do not actually celebrate most of these occasions. Rather they are used as a time to visit relatives, re-paper the sitting room, or catch up on all those little tasks that an ordinary weekend leaves incomplete. Even Christmas has expanded from the medieval twelve days to about four months, so that when the actual day arrives we have all become weary of the carols and Christmas tunes played everywhere, the messages on TV and the shops full of bright lights and expensive trinkets which will be forgotten or broken within a few days of their receipt. We need to reclaim our cycles of celebration, to make them mean something again.

People used to live their whole lives punctuated only by the phases of the Moon, the cycles of the Sun and the seasons of work in Nature's own timepiece. Now we are impelled by alarm clocks, bound by schedules, inhibited by artificial hours and minutes, to adhere to fixed periods of work, relaxation, sleep and pleasure. Long gone is the ability to work as long as the Sun shines, changing our jobs as the seasons alter, and when winter's dark lies over the land, to rest and withdraw, as do the trees and all living things subject to Nature's laws. This has further warped our inherent ability to mesh with the world so that time has become our enemy. We are under the thrall of Saturn's cruel scythe rather than using his sturdy stability as the foundation stones of an ever-changing life. Saturn or Chronos, the Lord of Time, should be our friend and supporter, yet through the imposition of false standards he has been eroded to a sort of death-like figure, who is feared and never called upon to fulfil his original function as the stabilizer and controller of boundaries.

Time has always passed, of course. People have grown up, died, and probably been reborn many times, as history has written in its book of years. Yet it was the monasteries who first began to chain themselves to the clock: prime, terce, sixt, nones, matins, compline – all the canonical hours which punctuated the days of monks and nuns throughout Christendom had to be regulated by bells, and from abbey to abbey. Simple clocks which worked by Nature began this process of regimentation: Sun dials, water clocks and candles marked the passing hours, burned away the days, cutting them into shreds. The common folk had no need for such divisions of their time – they rose with the Sun, ate when they were hungry (or had caught something for the pot), and slept when they were tired or it was too dark to continue with their work. But then the alien bells began to regulate their work too, gradually turning the freedom and timelessness into clock-divided periods of work, rest and play.

Similarly, the year, whose feasts were dictated by Mother Nature, fell under the rule of the Church. Dates for events began to be fixed by a calendar, dictated by kings and popes for the whole of the known world. Many of the old celebrations had been held at times when there was a specific thing to be happy about, for example, a harvest, the ending of winter or the birth of lambs. Today there are many modern pagans who regularly attend sabbats, but who have no inkling as to what Nature herself is offering her children. It is all very well knowing when the Feast of Imbolc or that of Samhain is, but this is of little use if it means nothing to your heart and feelings about the land and its own gifts. We all need to realign ourselves with the actual seasons and not blindly follow a calendar, which was designed for the convenience of keeping the Church's faithful in step with each other. We need to examine the symbols, the gifts, the associations with each festival as we come to celebrate it, so that it actually means something to us, as individuals or as members of a community. What, for example, do chocolate eggs, rabbits, chicks and yellow flowers have to do with the cruel death and resurrection of Jesus? Not a lot! They are, however, powerful pagan symbols of the life of the returning spring, celebrated even to this day in the English name of the feast, Easter, as Eostre was the Saxon name for the Goddess of Spring! In many other lands the name of this holiday (from holy day) is something to do with the Passion of Christ – Paques in French.

SPRING

In Britain the pagan festival of the Spring Goddess, around the time of the Spring Equinox at the end of March, was celebrated with painted and decorated eggs – symbols of the Life that was returning. There were also hares, not rabbits, for these are sacred to the Moon Goddess and are seldom eaten because witches were supposed to be able to turn into them when they shape-shifted. (This belief stems from a witness to a pagan gathering who, when asked whom he had seen replied, *'Only some hares playing in a field'* – a white lie to protect his friends or family!) Even the spicy hot-crossed buns have a pagan implication, for the sign of the cross within the circle to an astrologer (whose science is far older than Christianity), represents the planet Earth. This symbol links with the four directions, the four elements, the four seasons and so on, making it a magical talisman for balance and harmony at the time when the Sun recommences its journey around the Signs of the Zodiac.

The four seasons of the year, separated by ancient festivals, each has a particular energy associated with them which, as you become more sensitive to the natural rhythms of the year, will feel more obvious. Spring is the Sowing Tide, which is a fairly obvious one, when all green things are springing forth, renewed from their winter sleep – this is true in the Northern hemisphere, and the reverse is the case for the Southern hemisphere. It is a time of expansion, when the plans of the winter may be put forth into action, and all things can be brought into daylight as the seasons progress. It is a time of putting on new clothes, rejoicing in the flowers of garden and hedgerow, of wood or meadow, of getting out and about, renewing old friendships, beginning new ones, and finding ways to share your celebrations of the magic of renewal.

SUMMER

The summer brings the Growing Tide, when things come to fruition, ripen and fulfil the promises of spring. It is a time of completion and of sacrifice. Look at the

---

old song about John Barleycorn, how the barley which is a representative of all heroes, grows and is finally cut down, dried, winnowed, roasted and turned into barley malt and ale. The king is dead, long live the king, symbolically slain so that from his physical body – the grain – all the people shall be fed with bread. There are many harvest customs dating back a long way, which encapsulate the idea of the sacred king dying and being preserved, to rise not in three days, but in half a year as next spring's greenery. The rites at harvest are half in mourning for Lugh, the Sun God, whose waning light is perceived in the shortening days, and half in celebration of the harvest he has supplied. It is also a time of looking back on what has been achieved and what personal harvests have been reaped from enterprises other than in the agricultural field.

AUTUMN

Next comes the Harvesting or Reaping Tide, a time of inward turning as well as celebration. Many other harvests are gathered now, of fruit and olives, of grapes and the start of the wine-making process in warmer lands than Britain, although wine has always been made here from wild fruits and berries, as well as grapes, which are being grown in increasing quantities. It used to be a great time of co-operation, of celebration and of hard work to ensure that as much of every foodstuff as possible was carefully gathered in and preserved against the barren months of winter. Every apple had to be picked with care, every last ear of corn, barley, oats and rye gleaned by someone for use as food during the coming year. Every last olive was beaten from the trees into the cloths below to press for its dark oil, or to pickle for eating. Unless everyone within the community worked with a will, some precious commodity might be spoiled by the weather, or eaten by livestock, before it could be stacked safely in the barns.

Magically, it was a time of celebration, for once the hard work of harvesting was complete, the animals brought into their winter quarters and a few choice beasts slaughtered and preserved with salt, with smoke or pickled in brine to provide some meat for the winter, there would be a feast of the bits of meat that could not be preserved and the blood and offal would be made into sausages and special dishes according to local recipes.

WINTER

The last season brings the Cleansing Tide, from Yule to the Spring Equinox, when Nature sleeps and wraps her land in a new white quilt of snow, bares the tree branches, fills the streams with rain, and the wind cleanses the whole atmosphere. It is a season of thinking and planning, of discovering what has been achieved and what unfinished work can readily be cast away. It is a time when all things are washed clean or swept away. In the short days after the bright lights of Christmas there is a dark time; February is gloomy and everyone longs for the Sun. It is a time when things get cleared out of our lives, more people die at this season, depression is rife, gloom and doom seem to fill all the media. All these things are a natural response to the short days, the miserable weather and, in earlier times, the lack of vitamins in a diet often consisting only of bread, hard cheese and ale. We can overcome this feeling of depression, in part at least, by getting out into every moment of natural sunshine, or even plain daylight. We can fight back by taking extra vitamins D and A found in fish oils, especially halibut or cod liver oils, and by recognising that what we are feeling is a natural reaction of an animal to winter!

ATTUNING TO THE SEASONS
Once you start to attune yourself to the passing seasons you will find that life takes on a new vitality. If you feel down in the dumps it may be the time of year, not some ghastly problem which appears to be ruining your life. It will change for the better as soon as March ends, and the longer days start to be noticeable. As summer comes you will recognise the growth period in all your affairs, and see how they seem to blossom and promise the fruits to come. In the autumn you will start to reap the benefits of your earlier activities, and as winter brings a slowing down, there should be a feeling of completion and satisfaction in a job well done. Now you should

be able to see clearly what your year of labour in the physical, mental and magical fields has brought, what sort of harvest you have been able to gather into your storage areas, including those of increased knowledge and practical wisdom.

Magic, like growing trees, takes time. You cannot speed the growth of an oak, nor the accomplishment of your True Will, assuming you have found out what that is! You can only learn patience, and use the tides in your own favour, by being willing to sow and reap, and cast aside those things which are finished with, in order to make a growing medium for next year's cycle.

You have to be willing, at the Cleansing Tide, to pay your debts and settle the accounts for those things which require some kind of payment. Sometimes this can seem to be a time when things get swept out of your control, when friendships may end or when highly valued objects get broken or lost. It is a sad time, too, for many people, as others vanish from their lives forever, and half-completed projects may fall in ruins, love affairs end, or death takes away those you love and respect.

Each year is made up of four main sections, and at the start or end of each is a Festival. Some prefer to use those of the Old Gods, celebrating the Life Cycle of the Goddess of Earth and her consort, the Sun God – her son and lover. Others divide their year according to the Solar Feasts, at the solstices and equinoxes as the Sun enters a new section of the Zodiac. Many people begin their own year at their birthday, or at the local New Year, which could be January, the Winter Solstice, the Jewish New Year in September, the Chinese New Year in February, or the Solar New Year in March. In any case, it is not only the start of a year that is important, but what you can best do to mark the times and tides which matter to you or your family, in the ways in which your companions might choose to celebrate each of the time posts which divide the twelve calendar months, or almost thirteen lunar months.

If you are really going to become a walker in the Old Ways you will need to observe the lunar and solar dates, and the natural times of rejoicing or festival as they occur, not mere modern calendar dates, fixed by church or state. You will have to recognise that Nature is fickle, spring can come early or late, harvest time may vary from area to area, even the main harvest may differ, being wheat in one place, maize in another or fruit, grapes or olives somewhere else. There can be harvests of new livestock, fish, game or water fowl, each with a particular season and a particular time of prohibition. You might choose dates for your own celebrations which mark family birthdays or anniversaries, you might encourage your local community to rediscover traditional feasts and holy days dedicated to a village saint or hero. In many parts of Britain, at least, an interest in folk customs, Morris dancing and traditional celebrations, linked with the church or a natural spring of water, are being revived because it is recognised that many people enjoy sharing such events. They may bring in tourists or visitors, they may help unite a scattered community, or encourage young people to join in ancient festivities.

If you are pursuing your studies alone, in a city or built up area, you will have to observe other patterns of natural cycles in order to establish your own series of rituals or celebrations. These can vary from inviting a few friends round to a special meal, or a picnic with some children in a naturally beautiful place, at one of the dates you have selected, to the design and setting up of a small shrine in your garden, or indoors if all else fails. You do not need to stress the idea of a pagan feast, if you do not feel comfortable with that idea, nor should you ever do anything to impress your guests with your secret knowledge, for that is the path of folly; but a little thought about the food and drink, the place settings or table decorations can clearly indicate to the wise that this is not an ordinary birthday party.

The ancient Celts not only used trees as the names of their letters but named their months after them. There are quite a few variations on which of our modern months coincided with which Celtic ones, and there is not even a commonly held notion of which the first month was, although many scholars accept that the Celtic year began around November. It is also believed that they had a lunar calendar with thirteen months, and this is an easier way to sort out your own calendar if you want to build up a system into which you can begin to fit larger or more elaborate celebrations as time goes by.

Of course if you are already part of a group which has a series of sabbats or celebrations, you will have plenty of material to base your system on. It never hurts to understand thoroughly the reasons for any kind of seasonal or other feast. Many people, however, who belong to pagan groups, celebrate without having the faintest idea what it is all about. No one in the magical world should join in things they do not understand, for knowledge is power, and all rites require this to succeed. Even something as basic as a clearly defined festival, such as Hallowe'en, can have some sinister overtones unless you realise what is meant and what aspects of the Goddess are being invoked at that time.

It is probably best to start with each New Moon and see it as a time of commencement or renewal. Not only should you have a note of the date in your magical diary, but you should make it your personal act of dedication to Mother Nature to go out, just after sunset, and actually look for the New Moon low on the western horizon. It takes only a moment and shows that you are aware. The same applies at the first quarter, when the Moon looks like a 'D,' at the Full Moon, when she rises later at night; and the last quarter, when she rises after midnight. Find out exactly why the Moon's appearance alters night by night; and learn to recognize the phase at a glance, preferably from out of doors!

There are lots of old country calendars which give

quaint names to each lunar month, but you can easily select your own based on the weather, the occurrences of wild flowers, the return or departure of migrating birds or animals, or even family birthdays or anniversaries. Anything in magic which you 'make up', design or are inspired to use – be it a festival, an instrument or a magical robe – will be a much more potent thing than one that someone else has created. It should always be your Will which dictates what should be used and when. Only by allowing yourself to make decisions –and to be wrong occasionally – is your knowledge and confidence going to expand. Being wrong, making mistakes and tripping over are great teaching processes and should not be feared. After all the man who never made any mistakes never made anything at all!

You can find suitable names for the New Moon for each month of the year. For example, beginning in November, the New Moon could be called Leaf Fall Moon: in December, the name could be First Frost Moon: in January, Snowfall Moon: in February, Light Spring Moon: in March, Wind Tossed Moon: in April, Flower-Shower Moon: in May, White Lady Moon: in long-lighted June, Sunshine Moon: in July, Field Poppy Moon: in August, as the corn ripens, Wheat Wind Moon: in September, traditionally there is the Harvest Moon: and finally in October, Hunter's Moon, although the last two are the names given to the Full, rather than the New Moon phase.

These seasons are those of the southern part of

England. Obviously in other lands the prevailing weather will vary, and also each year will be different. If you have a steady weather pattern you may seek out other names. Often they turn up in old agricultural accounts, and gypsies and other pagan or wandering peoples may have a separate calendar, which you could adopt as the basis for your own. Do some research. Most libraries have books on calendar customs from which you will be able to discover all sorts of feasts and festivals in your own locality, and old maps will indicate holy wells, springs, old trackways, field names, standing stones and much more that is linked with ancient rituals or customs, if you bother to find out.

Consider local place names, too, for these may relate to old fairs, which happened each year when livestock was sold, or farm workers hired. There used to be local Horse Fairs, Horn Fairs (when all sorts of horned animals were sold, including cattle and rams), Goose Fairs, Strawberry Fairs, and often within the overall selling of animals or produce, there were horse-races, competitions for decorating things, craftworkers' demonstrations, and ox or ram roasts, as well as stalls dispensing ale, beer and cider in vast quantities. Some of these ancient fairs were recalled in songs, like Widdecombe Fair in Devon, or Scarborough Fair in Yorkshire, and the folk song about the Derby Ram. There is a mass of material which can help you uncover aspects of the folk traditions and gatherings to be found in old local archives, folk songs and forgotten traditional events, if you delve about in the reference library. On your own you might not be able to do a lot to celebrate these old public feasts, but you can experiment with traditional recipes for cakes and wines, for special roasts or regional cheeses. Throughout the year in Britain, there are dozens of special foods, local delicacies, or seasonal produce which can be eaten with recollection of Mother Nature's bounty, or in remembrance of some traditional feast day. From Christmas pudding and mince pies (both originally savouries), through to Easter's hot-crossed buns and simnel cake, lenten loaves, Shrove Tuesday pancakes, and all the seasons of freshwater fish, wild fowl and game, like venison and hares, Michaelmas Fairings and many other special treats.

There are whole books of recipes which can be tested. You can also discover where there are public gatherings to mark the seasons, such as the Midsummer Morris Ring meetings, when dozens of sides of Morris Men – and these days, Women – gather to dance and sing in many towns around the country. There are Well Blessing or Dressing Festivals, the 'Gloucester Cheese Rolling Ritual' - which encourages the return of the Spring Sun – as well as pancake races, with a similar magical significance, often lost on the bewildered audience who flock to watch. There may be a Crowning of the May Queen, or a Hobby Horse Festival, or a Time of Blessing the Boats and Nets of fisherfolk, or the Horses on Epsom Downs.

Each of these preserves the half-forgotten fragments

of ancient rituals to which our ancestors would have walked many miles to attend in honour of Nature and her seasonal gifts. From Cornwall to the Hebrides, from Kent to Cumbria there are bonfires, races, burning ships or effigies, processions of Christian or pagan origins, yet underlying the modern facade is an ancient and powerful ceremony being performed, which you can perceive once you begin to know what to look for, and your senses are awakened to all about you.

ANCIENT FESTIVALS

If you want to join in the pattern of pagan feasts which are celebrated by many of today's witches, you will have eight, or nine, festivals in the older calendar to look forward to each year. This section focuses on those in Great Britain but every other country has its own. You may only be in a position to decorate a corner of your living space with seasonal symbols or flowers and greenery, for example, or you may have an area in or out of doors which may be designated an 'altar' – though this does not have to be a table, it could be a flower bed, a statue or a bird table – which you make as the centre piece of your offering to Nature. Perhaps you could design a circular space, edged with white pebbles or sea shells as a kind of permanent Magical Circle, around which you can move the direction of attention with the Sun throughout the turning year, as was traditional among followers of the Old Religion. Each festival is linked with a particular direction or point of the compass, and at that time a special energy or current would be felt to flow, as if the Earth's own energy patterns changed with the passing months.

If you begin around the middle of winter your focus will be to the North. It is the time of the Rebirth of the Sun, the Sacred Son of the Earth Mother, born in the longest night in a cave. Most people are familiar with the idea of decorating their houses with green branches of holly with its scarlet berries – long associated with the magic of life – and with ivy, the twining stems of which represent the binding power of the Earth Mother linking all things together. The decorated tree, a modern introduction on old roots, long sacred to the Norse folk, and lit with candles, tinsel and baubles, like sacred fruits, is another traditional symbol of life returning in the winter's dark. The fairy or angel on the top is the Lady herself, Virgin Mother of a Divine Child, Mother of God, or Earth Mother, as you will.

The most frequently overlooked festival in the ancient calendar is that of Twelfth Night, the Feast of Epiphany, when the Three Wise Men –- Astrologer Kings – arrived with their magical gifts of gold, frankincense and myrrh. This echoes the pagan rite in Britain when the Goddess names and arms her Son, the Solar Hero. She offers him symbols of magic, priesthood and kingship, just as the Three Kings offered the infant Jesus gold for temporal power, frankincense for religious power and myrrh as a token of the sacrifice to come. In the traditional pagan ceremony a young man acts out the Sun God and an older woman, his Mother. In some instances a special cake is baked with a mark across the top and tokens hidden in it – men's on one side, and women's on the other – so that the various parts of the seasonal rite are cast by lot, the Goddess allowing each person to find the right symbol in their slice of cake.

The next pagan festival is Candlemas at the beginning of February, or the Feast of St Bride, a Christian version of Brigid, the Goddess of springs of water, who is honoured with the Bride's Bed. In Ireland and other places, the women of the community deck out a special place beside the hearth with bright ribbons and cloths, and the earliest spring flowers – usually snowdrops or violets. Each in turn bows to the Goddess who is invited to be present, and pours an offering of wine, milk or spring water, and then each asks for a special kind of blessing on her activities during the coming year. The men are then allowed to come into the special place and, after paying for entry by either a token – like a pine cone or small coin – or a kiss, they also make an offering and ask a favour of the Goddess.

After everyone has asked for their gift, candles are lit to make the pattern of a star in honour of the Star Child, the Son of the Goddess. Today these are usually small night-lights because they are reasonably safe, but in earlier times long tapers might have been stuck into the earth floor of the house, or into a bowl of earth.

In another version of the ritual a young girl representing the Virgin Mother Goddess, hooded and cloaked in black, enters the room of people and each one whispers to her their needs or desires. Offerings are also made by pouring libations or setting out posies of flowers that have been gathered that day. After she has been greeted by each member of the group her dark cloak is removed and under it she is dressed in either light green or white. She carries a dish of flowers set with a lighted candle, which she has hidden under her cloak as a symbol of the Light which never dies. All the candles set about the room are then lit from that flame.

The next festival usually celebrated is the Spring Equinox, on about 21 March, though like all these festivals the actual date may shift a day or two. In earlier times. this was the actual time of seed-sowing, and the appearance of many wild and spring flowers, particularly yellow ones in Britain, seemed to honour the Sun God. Now, at about Lady Day, he is ready to prove his virility, and after dancing his way through the Circle of the Zodiac, he sets off into the world to be the Champion of the Goddess, his mother and lover, brandishing the spear which is his symbol of power. (Lady Day is about 25 March, nine months before Yule!) Seeds are often blessed and then mixed with the rest of the corn before it is sown in the fields. Now it is time to greet the Sunrise of the Year, looking East.

At the beginning of the month of May when, and only when, the hawthorn is bursting into blossom, you can celebrate May Day. Adopted as a sort of national festival day in Russia – among other places – Beltane, the Feast of the Good Fires, marks the start of the summer season. In many villages, before the Reformation, the May Day festivities involved all kinds of wild celebrations and wearing of the green, a symbol of the Goddess, otherwise thought unlucky. Similarly, branches of flowering May, the sweet-scented hawthorn blooms, are allowed into the house on this day only, otherwise they are taboo. A May Queen, usually a young schoolgirl of grace, beauty and charm, is chosen and she rides through the streets on a flower-decked cart accompanied by Robin Hood or the Green Man – the pagan God of Nature in another guise. Dances round the May Pole with coloured ribbons bind the strength of the growing Sun into the land. It is a time of weddings and merry-making, and in earlier times the brides, like the Goddess, were already pregnant before they were wed. In the ritual, the Goddess's representative is disguised or shape-shifted into the form of a doe and is chased through the woods by the God in his form of hunter until, under the branches of the flowering May he catches her, and leads her back to the village. There they wed by jumping over the bonfire. The sacred direction is south-east.

Bonfires are important, for they were lit in May to burn special herbs which would purify and protect the cattle and sheep who were then driven out into the unfenced pastures for the summer. This was partly a magical act, and partly a real attempt at health care. They were also branded or marked by their owners, and the younger folk would spend the next six months following the livestock among the hills in search of good grazing, whilst hay was mown on the low land meadows, and corn tended in the fertile fields. The cattle herders would build simple bothies of wattle, or live in caves during the summer, keeping warm with a comely cow girl at night (or as women chose their own mates according to Celtic law, they would decide who to give their favours to). May Day rites take place around mid-morning.

Midsummer, the feast of the shortest night, or the Summer Solstice was a time of outdoor activities. Bringing in the hay and peat, tending green crops, shearing sheep, and working in field and orchard to weed and improve conditions for the harvests to come, would all have filled the days from May Day onwards, but Midsummer was the chance to celebrate all the hard work. There are many old customs involving Midsummer Bonfires: they are lit to this day on Cornish hill tops, there is dancing in the streets, and garden fetes, village festivals and sports days are held. It is a time of blessing the Sun God if his face has shone upon the half-year's labours, and a time to exhort him to greater things if his light has been clouded, and the skies have shed continuous rain.

The sacred direction is south, and the time is noonday. Now the healing power pours from the Sun, and the long light evenings offer the opportunities for strolling in the countryside, getting to know the full-leafed trees, the profusions of wild flowers now making a comeback. There are also many pick-your-own fruit farms open so that you can stock up on fresh strawberries, blackcurrants, gooseberries and raspberries, each in their season, and select the best vegetables, now often organically grown. There are farm parks where the children may meet cows, sheep, goats and horses, and find out where milk, cheese and wool originate from. Although these are artificial ways of encountering aspects of the agricultural cycle, they do at least provide the information, the understanding of the ancient processes by which the people are wedded to the land, and how each is dependent on the other.

Lammas Tide brings Wakes Week, and the first harvests of wheat, oats and barley in the south. It is a festival of both joy and sadness. The Corn God is cut down, his corn ground to make flour, or roasted to make malted barley for beer. There are many old traditions being maintained and revived which celebrate the harvest, for example, making corn dollies, in which the life force of the Sun is captured and kept indoors until the sowing time again, carefully woven to the local pattern, bound with red ribbons and set above the hearth – the house altar. It is a time of hard labour yet also of achievement, for when the corn fields are bare and the harvest is garnered into the barns, there is a tangible way of seeing what the powers of growth and light have wrought. The Corn God is slain and rests in the arms of his Earth Mother, and the Sun begins to wane, shortening the days again. The afternoon ritual faces south-west.

In September, when day and night are once more in balance at the Autumn Equinox, the other harvests are brought in: grapes in Italy, France and Spain, and apples, pears and the wild berries of elder, whortles, blackberries, sloes and damsons, from many of which powerful potions and heady wines, cider and liqueurs may be distilled in the long nights of winter. St Michael is a most pagan saint whose churches in high places remind us that in a previous incarnation he was the Sun God. When the hedges and gardens are misted with purple Michaelmas daisies with their strange fragrance, and the Michaelmas Goose fattens in the harvest fields – it is a time of Harvest Home, of feasting and bragging, or counting the bags of grain, the bales of hay and straw, the silage and the green crops, to keep the cattle through the winter. Churches hum with produce and the familiar hymns are sung: '*All is safely gathered in...*', '*We plough the fields and scatter the good seed on the land...*'. Each of us must also gather in our own harvest of ideas, of finished projects, or unfinished tasks. We must be ready to store those good ideas and cast out others which have outlived their usefulness.

The next festival is that of Hallowe'en, or Samhain, the Celtic summer's end. It is a time of potent magic, of the coming forth of old powers when the gates of the year open upon both the past and the future. Light is waning yet there is a rising tide of a deep, strong energy, flowing like a wild river through the Earth. As the trees scatter their leaves to the four winds, and the first frosts turn the grass from green to grey, it is a time of returning home, preparing for winter, and delving deep within yourself for the roots of new ideas. Publicly, it is a time of trick or treat, of disguises, of ghosts and ghouls, witches and fortune-telling and consulting old oracles in dark mirrors. The family all gather again, quitting their bothies in the hills, bringing the new babies, and telling tales of life in the wild. There are the stories of those who have passed through the gates of death, too, and a great feast, when those from the past are invited to share their wisdom, and those unborn, from the future, may come and meet their new parents. All look out to the north-west throughout the evening. .

Many of the games played at children's Hallowe'en parties –bobbing for apples, roasting chestnuts until they burst, looking in mirrors by candle-light at midnight to see your future lover, eating black foods and dressing up – are all parts of a very ancient pagan rite at this time. The disguises are to ward off any evil spirits who might recognise you if your face was not blacked with soot, or whose harmful influences are deflected because you are wearing your clothes inside out and back to front, when you return to your family home. Now the doors are

---

189

open and a great fire lit, within and without, to welcome home the souls of the dear departed, and even the sacred ancestors, back to the First Parents who begot all living people long ago. The best food and wine is set out in their honour, and songs and mimes tell the story of the turning year. There is plenty of material from which you can design your own personal ritual or celebration if you examine the folklore and old customs.

Last of all we come to Yule Tide, in fact three separate festivals that are rolled into one by most people. There is the Winter Solstice, when the Sun enters Capricorn, a precise moment in sidereal time. Then, there is Yule, the longest night of the year, when in darkness and silence the Sun is reborn in a cave deep inside the Earth Mother. Finally, there is Christmas, the birth of the Christ Child on 25 December, previously the Birthday of Mithras, the Persian Sun God. This date was chosen as a festival because as each day gets longer by about three minutes in southern Britain, four days after the Solstice it showed that the days were actually getting longer, so that the prayers, bonfires, candle-lit processions up the sacred hill, and all the magical spells had indeed worked, and lured the light of the Sun to return. Jesus was probably born in March!

The symbols associated with the season – the green branches, the decorated tree, the giving of presents, indulging the whims of children, visiting special places of entertainment, going to church and the Druidic mistletoe under which kisses are given and received – all echo much older practices. If you are able to strip away the dreadful commercialism. the materialism and the flashy exterior, there is a beautiful and meaningful feast at the bottom of it. You can certainly burn the Yule Log which is the great root of an oak set in the hearth to burn for the twelve days of Christmas. It is lit from the previous year's remains which have been carefully saved for the occasion, and its fertilizing ashes are later scattered on the fields. On it you can cast a written prayer for health and success, love and joy in the coming twelve months, or a token of those things you choose to discard.

You can decorate your house with all the old symbols and invite the Red Coated Sun God – Odin from the North or Bran from Wales – to enter your dwelling and fill it with light. You can welcome St Nicholas, if you so wish, with his companion, Black Pete, who fills your shoes with gifts, drinks the schnapps and eats the festive cake baked for him, as others do in some parts of Europe, in the early part of December. Or if you prefer, venture out at midnight on Christmas Eve to a dark stable and see if the horses and cows kneel in honour of the Goddess and her new born Child of Promise, according to the folk legend. There are dozens of surviving customs woven among the meaningless happenings of this now materialistic festival, and you can redeem those fragments of the Old Ways if you choose – honouring the Lady as Virgin Mother, eating her special feast of roast pork with honey, sharing her cake filled with rich spices, butter, sweet fruits and nuts with all your loved ones, retelling the hero tales, and singing the traditional carols in honour of the Old Gods: *'the rising of the Sun and the running of the deer, sweet calling of the merry birds, stars shining in the air ... of all the trees that are in the wood the Holly bears the crown.'*

It will depend on how you feel about celebrations whether you are in a position to share these with friends or a group of some sort. If you already belong to a coven, you will have your year mapped out for you, but it really is worth the effort of discovering how the cogs of nature turn, step by step, facing a new direction, holding a feast at a different moment of the day, experiencing how the Lord of the Wild and the Lady, Mother Nature, interact and bring forth their magical child, laying down secretly the underlying reasons for the celebration of many rites throughout the year. Look for the seasonal recipes, the symbols which are part of modern survivals, the activities of people who work with the land and its varied produce. Feel what the earth beneath your feet is doing, enact the older practices by sowing your parsley seeds on Good Friday and pouring boiling water over them to speed their germination, and learn to weave corn dollies, which can also be made out of rushes, or lavender stems if you have not found a source of tall wheat stalks (although you can grow your own out of pigeon corn!).

Immerse yourself in old customs, be they local revivals or undying feasts which have never been eroded by time or the Reformation – or even Victorian propriety. (This sentiment tried to do away with the wilder aspects of the Padstow Hobby Horse festival, for example, originally a fertility rite, in which a black stallion's skin was trooped about the town, soaking people symbolically with water. The local vicar tried to replace it with an ox roast and dance, but the local folk stuck to their black horse and his magical powers!) Explore the archives, the newspaper files and the library records for old events which may have some bearing on ancient customs, holy wells, agricultural practices and local celebrations – for they must have meant something once, and could again if we are able to stand back and recognise their value. Feasts were the cement which bound communities together and familiarised all the children with their neighbours, among whom they could feel safe. They punctuated the turning year with joy and laughter, and excuses for fun and games of all sorts; but now we have lost much of this simple heritage, and its loss is being felt by many, on quite a deep subconscious level. From an arrangement of flowers on a bookcase to a large outdoor festival involving the entire population of a village, each of the nine or so feasts can be celebrated, and begin to mean something to you again. You can attune yourself to the energy of each growing Moon, perceiving her effects upon your dreams and visions, knowing what particular power she represents at each cycle. Try to act by the tides and times, be they the swift ones of the Moon, or the longer solar and Earth cycles, celebrating the success of a harvest, the opening of some of the sacred flowers, the actual day of the first butterfly, or the day when the geese or starlings depart; always go by what Nature says and not a man-made calendar.

Always feel the energy, sense it, meditate upon it – do not just read someone else's account of what ought to be. Invent poetry for each feast from Moon-led inspiration, or from a clear eye and a free heart, rejoice in the good things, learn from the bad, and participate fully in the life of the Earth, ever-changing, ever-renewing herself; feeding us with the fruits of the seasons, fascinating us with the ever-changing sky, delighting us with the colours of wild flowers. Mother Nature cares.

End Word

WILD WITCHCRAFT is part of our inheritance: a part we have through our natural connection with all the inhabitants of planet Earth; a part we can explore and redevelop by dedicated effort and hard work. The arts and crafts of magic require just as much hard work and consistent effort as do any other skills, technological knowledge and practical activities. No one can sell you wisdom or power unless you pay for these by the work of your own hands, brain and soul.

Today we have become detached from the natural cycles of the Earth, we have become over-greedy for her bounty, we have become careless with those treasures she has so freely bestowed upon us, her children. Only by making a conscious effort to realign ourselves with the tides and times of the planet, and by gently re-awakening those old powers we all have access to, can we hope to survive as a race or species in this polluted world. We have to relearn many old skills, many ancient techniques, but these do not require expensive equipment, elaborate temples, arcane instruments. They require our own, individual commitment to the process of learning. We each have myriad skills and hidden abilities at our beck and call if we take time to discover what they are, and then retrain them so that they serve us.

We need to put aside the trappings of the modern world, learn who we are as unique beings, where we have come from and where we most desire to go. Only by living in the real world can we begin to appreciate, and then explore, those other worlds which are so immanent, yet seem so far away and hard to attain. We have to have a firm and solid foundation in this place, in this body and in this time before we can safely launch our wills and consciousness into other realms. There is no way we can buy entry to those worlds.

Initiation will not automatically open the hidden doors to the occult, in fact in many cases, those who go through a ritual of initiation unprepared and untrained, so firmly shut the doors to those secret paths that they may never be able to find them even if they receive correct instruction and knowledge later on. No one can give you a free pass, nor can you decide from your own power or knowledge, to start ordering beings from other levels of reality about, or commanding Elementals or Angels to do your bidding. They are much older, wiser and bigger than we are, and far more potent on the inner ways.

Wild Witchcraft is a lonely path. You have to seek out

the Old Gods where they dwell, visit them humbly with the right offerings, and go to their realms as children. You need to cultivate the skills of perception, imagination and vision that you had as a child. Learn to play at the games of mind and awareness which will open the gates to intuition, creativity and focused inner sight. Know when and where to begin these games, and when to stop and put away the toys of magic, the sensitivity of psychism and the childlike freedom of spirit.

Learn to love, appreciate and understand the patterns and power of Mother Nature herself. Wholeheartedly throw your self into conservation, ecology and a thorough knowledge of what is good for the world – and all its people – and what is essentially harmful. Not only in the world outside but by spiritual ecology, by gardening within your mind, and making the wasteland within green and fertile. Learn from the mistakes you have made, see them as valuable experiences, not fearful, black images which need to be shoved into the darkest corner of your memory. There they will rot and fester, and produce nasty side-effects which will come and haunt you, in the days to come. Learn from the mistakes of others, too, so that you do not fall into that kind of folly.

Be patient, and accept that true knowledge grows slowly, organically, as do oak trees and the paths of rivers. Wisdom is as old as human consciousness, and magic only a few years younger. You cannot expect to gain these things in a few weeks of desultory work. You need many years of continuous effort so that your magic is under your control, and all the doors you open can be safely and firmly closed at your will.

Strive always to know yourself better, and so become more aware and sympathetic to others. Understand their needs as well as your own, turn your back on selfishness, and the short, deadly road to anti-evolutionary magic. Be silent about those secrets which the Earth herself has taught you. Be respectful to all beings you encounter on your inner journeys. Earn love, by loving what you are and what you may become, and strive for the best with all your being. Earn honour and become self-confident by your actions and love for the world. You cannot buy power, or respect, or assistance unless you are worthy. Seek always to rise upwards so that you may serve Creation through serving Nature.

The Lord and the Lady bring you to the accomplishment of your true Will, the Great Work, the summum bonum. True Wisdom and Perfect Happiness.

THE DRUID WAY
By Philip Carr-Gomm

In *The Druid Way*, Philip Carr-Gomm takes us on a journey through the sacred landscape of Southern Britain, and as he does so, we learn about Druidry as a living tradition of the land and its people, a tradition that is as relevant today as it was for our ancestors.

As we walk the ancient tracks across the South Downs we encounter dragons and giants, ancestral voices and ancient places that speak to us of the beauty of a spiritual way that still exists and can still be followed. We learn how Druidry can help us to sense again our kinship with Nature, and how following the Druid Way can lead us towards a profound sense of oneness with all life.

This new edition has been extensively revised and includes the complete ceremonies of three Rites of Passage, a guide to the sacred sites of Sussex and a Foreword by Cairisthea Worthington.

'This whole book is a delight. It is the diary of a sacred journey, through sacred space, and through the heart and mind – a book to use, to keep and to remember.'
Wood & Water

'This book provides inspiration, soul-food and encouragement to those who long to be part of the richer life of this beautiful planet.'
CAITLIN MATTHEWS

ISBN 978-1-870450-62-1

THE GRAIL SEEKER'S COMPANION
By John Matthews & Marian Green

There have been many books about the Grail, written from many differing standpoints. Some have been practical, some purely historical, others literary, but this is the first Grail book which sets out to help the esoterically inclined seeker through the maze of symbolism, character and myth which surrounds the central point of the Grail.

In today's frantic world when many people have their material needs met some still seek spiritual fulfilment. They are drawn to explore the old philosophies and traditions,particularly that of our Western Celtic Heritage. It is here they encounter the quest for the Holy Grail, that mysterious object which will bring hope and healing to all. Some have
come to recognise that they dwell in a spiritual wasteland and now search that symbol of the Grail which may be the only remedy. Here is the guide book for the modern seeker,explaining the history and pointing clearly towards the Aquarian Grail of the future. John Matthews and Marian Green have each been involved in the study of the mysteries of Britain and the Grail myth for over thirty-five years.

In *The Grail Seeker's Companion* they have provided a guidebook not just to places, but to people, stories and theories surrounding the Grail. A reference book of Graliology, including history, ritual, meditation, advice and instruction. In short, everything you are likely to need before you set out on the most important adventure of your life.

'This is the only book that points the way to the Holy Grail in the 21st century.' *Quest*

ISBN 978-1-870450-49-2

THE WESTERN MYSTERY TRADITION
Christine Hartley

A reissue of a classic work, by a pupil of Dion Fortune, on the mythical and historical roots of Western occultism. Christine Hartley's aim was to demonstrate that we in the West, far from being dependent upon Eastern esoteric teachings, possess a rich and potent mystery tradition of our own, evoked and defined in myth, legend, folklore and song, and embodied in the legacy of Druidic culture.

More importantly, she provides practical guidelines for modernstudents of the ancient mysteries, 'The Western Mystery Tradition,' in Christine Hartley's view, 'is the basis of the Western religious feeling, the foundation of our spiritual life, the matrix of our religious formulae, whether we are aware of it or not. To it we owe the life and force of our spiritual life.'

ISBN 978-1-870450-24-9

A MODERN MAGICIAN'S HANDBOOK
Marian Green

This book presents the ancient arts of magic, ritual and practical occult arts as used by modern ceremonial magicians and witches in a way that everyone can master, bringing them into the Age of Aquarius. Drawing on over three decades of practical experience, Marian Green offers a simple approach to the various skills and techniques that are needed to turn an interest into a working knowledge of magic.

Each section offers explanations, guidance and practical exercises in meditation, inner journeying, preparation for ritual, the arts of divination and many more of today's esoteric practices. No student is too young or too old to benefit from the material set out for them in this book, and its simple language may help even experienced magicians and witches understand their arts in greater depth.

ISBN 978-1-870450-43-0

Marian Green and J. Matthews, *The Grail Seeker's Companion*, Thoth Publications.

Christine Hartley, *The Western Mystery Tradition*, Thoth Publications.

Murry Hope, P*ractical Egyptian Magic*, Thoth Publications.

Practical Techniques of Psychic Self-Defence, Aquarian.

Naomi Humphrey, *Meditation – the Inner Way*, Aquarian.

Ronald Hutton, *The Triumph of the Moon*, Oxford University Press, 1999

Witches, Druids and King Arthur, Hambledon & London, 2003

Carl Jung, *Memories, Dreams, Reflections*, Fontana.

Gareth Knight, *The Secret Tradition in Arthurian Legend*, Aquarian.

T. C. Lethbridge, *Ghost and Divining Rod*.

Caitlin Matthews, *Mabon and the Mysteries of Britain*, Arkana, RKP.

Caitlin and John Matthews, *The Western Way*, Vols. I and II, Arkana, RKP.

John and Caitlin Matthews, *Hallowquest*, Aquarian.

The Arthurian Tarot Course, Aquarian.

Naomi Ozaniec, *Daughter of the Goddess*, Aquarian.

Will Parfitt, *The Living Qabalah*, Element.

Nigel Pennick, *Practical Magic in the Northern Tradition*, Thoth Publications.

Israel Regardie, *The Complete Golden Dawn*, Aquarian..

Alan Richardson, *Introduction to the Mystical Qabalah*, Aquarian.

Priestess (biography of Dion Fortune), Thoth Publications.

Starhawk, *The Spiral Dance*, Weiser, USA.

R. J. (Bob) Stewart, *Living Magical Arts*, Thoth Publications.

Advanced Magical Arts, Thoth Publications.

Power Within the Land, Element.

Val Thomas, *Of Chalk and Flint: A Way of Norfolk Magic*, Troy Books 2019

Doreen Valiente, *ABC of Witchcraft*, Hale.

Natural Magic, Hale.

Witchcraft for Tomorrow, Hale.

Much fiction is magical – try these authors: Terry Pratchett, Alan Garner, Ben Aaronavitch, Christopher Fowler, Ursula Le Guin, Phil Rickman, Elly Griffiths

BIBLIOGRAPHY

Many of the authors whose works are listed below have written a number of similar books, but these are the most helpful to novices. New books are always being published, so write to the publishers for a catalogue if there is no good bookshop near you.

Margot Adler, *Drawing Down the Moon*, USA.

Rae Beth, *Hedge Witch*, Hale, 2002.

J. H. Brennan, *Astral Doorways*, Thoth Publications.

W. E. Butler, *Apprenticed to Magic*, Thoth Publications.

Lords of Light, Destiny Books, USA.

Philip Carr-Gomm, *The Druid Way*, Thoth Publications.

The Book of English Magic, John Murray, 2009.

Melita Denning and Osbourne Phillips, *Planetary Magick*, Llewellyn USA.

Dion Fortune, *The Magical Battle of Britain*, Thoth.

The Sea Priestess (Novel), Aquarian.

The Training and Work of an Initiate, Aquarian.

Sir James Frazer, *The Golden Bough*.

G. B. Gardner, *The Meaning of Witchcraft*.

Witchcraft Today.

W. G. Gray, *Ladder of Lights*, Aquarian.

Tom Graves, *The Diviner's Handbook*, Aquarian.

Towards a Magical Technology, Aquarian.

Marian Green, *The Gentle Arts of Natural Magic*, Thoth Publications.

A Witch Alone, Aquarian.

A Calendar of Festivals, Element.

Practical Techniques of Modern Magic, Thoth Publications.

Charms, Amulets, Talismans and Spells, Wooden Books, 2018.

The Apprentice Witch's Spellbook, Quarto Publishing, 2018.

An Introduction to Spiritual Ecology, The Crowood Press, 2022

The Treasure of the Silver Web (Novel), Thoth Publications.

THE ARTHURIAN FORMULA
By Dion Fortune, Margaret Lumley Brown & Gareth Knight

The Arthurian Formula, was the last major work of Dion Fortune, and formed the corner stone of the inner work of her Society of the Inner Light for the following twenty years, supplemented by the remarkably gifted psychic Margaret Lumley Brown. It later formed the basis for work by Gareth Knight with the Company of Hawkwood and allied groups in later years, inspiring his book *The Secret Tradition in Arthurian Legend*.

Dion Fortune's contribution explores the remote sources of the Arthurian legends and the mission of Merlin, played out in the polar relationships between Arthur, Guenevere and Lancelot in both human and faery dynamics, and leading to aspects of the Grail. Margaret Lumley Brown develops the threads in the labyrinth formed by the archetypal patterns of the knights and ladies, including particular reference to Morgan le Fay. Gareth Knight's commentary pulls together these strands with an overview of the various traditions back of the Arthurian Formula – of Glastonbury, Atlantis, the world of Faery, Merlin, the Troubadours, the cult of Queen Venus, and their application in the practical Mysteries of today.

An introductory commentary by Gareth Knight includes a guide to recent academic and esoteric scholarship and is supplemented by Appendices on the Glastonbury legends, clairvoyant impressions of Atlantis, (from which archetypal principles behind the Arthurian legends are held ultimately to spring) and a remarkable perspective on Queen Gwenevere and the Faery and Grail traditions, by Wendy Berg.

ISBN 978-1-870450-90-4

THE WITCH'S JOURNEY
By Moira Hodgkinson

Drawing on the experience and practice of over Twenty-five years, the author celebrates the God and Goddess and the pagan ways of a living, everyday witchcraft.

There are ceremonies, unique invocations and ideas for journey work to deepen your connection with the archetypal deities of witchcraft, The male and female mysteries and rites of passage are explored to honour the divine within and rituals are given as inspiration to mark different phases of life, such as coming of age and parenthood.

The book gives information on useful healing techniques, with examples of try out for yourself and others. Learn how to make your own casting stones for divination and find meaningful symbols you can relate to easily for readings.

There is an informative section on solar magic as well as looking at the moon in-depth and there are new ideas and tips to celebrate the Sabbats with friends, family or a group, Spell craft, pathworking and reverence combine in this valuable book to augment your skills and create genuine connections to the energies that are all around us.

The Witch's Journey is perfect for anyone who wants that little bit more from their magical world.

ISBN – 9781870450768

PRACTICAL ATLANTEAN MAGIC
By Murry Hope

This book will take you on a journey through the mystical, psychological and psychic evidence of the existence of Atlantis and all that it has stood for within the Collective Consciousness of human culture through the ages. Subjects covered include – the legend of Atlantis, facts and fictions, the Atlantean basis of western magic, the peoples and priesthood of Atlantis, Stellar and solar magic, lessons, exercises, prayers and rites.

ISBN 978 1 870450 57 7

PRACTICAL CELTIC MAGIC
By Murry Hope

This enchanting book covers the ethnic and indigenous backgrounds of the Celtic race as well as the oral tradition upon which its mystique was built. Surrounded by an aura of romanticism and fantasy, the Celts continue to fascinate us, and here Murry Hope carefully examines their beliefs concerning religion, mysticism and magic, drawing us into their world of Gods and Goddesses, bringing us to the practical Celtic magic
for today's world.

ISBN 978 1 870450 720

THE PSYCHOLOGY OF RITUAL
By Murry Hope
Both the therapeutic benefits of ritual and its potential as a conditioning agent have been realised by mankind for ages. Murry Hope examines the birth, growth and history of the rite, as well as its influence on cultural
development over the centuries.

ISBN 978 1 870450 19 5

www.ingramcontent.com/pod-product-compliance
Lightning Source LLC
Chambersburg PA
CBHW071953090426
42740CB00011B/1919

* 9 7 8 1 9 1 3 6 6 0 4 1 3 *